W9-AKV-664

VIKTOR E. FRANKL M.D., Ph.D. is Professor of Neurology and Psychiatry at the University of Vienna Medical School and Distinguished Professor of Logotherapy at the U.S. International University in California. He is the founder of what has come to be called the Third Viennese School of Psychotherapy (after Freud's psychoanalysis and Adler's individual psychology)—the school of logotherapy. This system is based upon the belief that man seeks meaning, and that discovering the special significance in one's life is a psychologically healing process. Professor Frankl received the degrees of Doctor of Medicine and Doctor of Philosophy from the University of Vienna. During World War II he spent three years at Auschwitz, Dachau and other concentration camps. Dr. Frankl first published in 1924 in the *International Journal of Psychoanalysis* and has since published twenty-eight books which have been translated into many languages. His book *Man's Search for Meaning* has sold more than two and a half million copies. Dr. Frankl is the president of the Austrian Medical Society of Psychotherapy, and has been a frequent guest lecturer and visiting professor at universities throughout the world. He has received sixteen honorary doctorates, as well as the American Psychiatric Association's Oskar Pfister Award and Lifetime Achievement Award of the Foundation for Hospice and Homecare.

VIKTOR E. FRANKL

THE
WILL
TO
MEANING

FOUNDATIONS AND APPLICATIONS OF LOGOTHERAPY

EXPANDED EDITION

A MERIDIAN BOOK

MERIDIAN
Published by the Penguin Group
Penguin Books USA Inc., 375 Hudson Street,
New York, New York 10014, U.S.A.
Penguin Books Ltd, 27 Wrights Lane, London W8 5TZ, England
Penguin Books Australia Ltd, Ringwood, Victoria, Australia
Penguin Books Canada Ltd, 10 Alcorn Avenue, Toronto,
Ontario, Canada, M4V 3B2
Penguin Books (N.Z.) Ltd, 182–190 Wairau Road, Auckland 10,
New Zealand

Penguin Books Ltd, Registered Offices:
Harmondsworth, Middlesex, England

Published by Meridian, an imprint of Dutton Signet, a division of
Penguin Books USA Inc.

First Plume Printing, March, 1970
First Meridian Printing, (Expanded Edition), September, 1988
14 13 12 11 10 9 8 7

Copyright © 1969, 1988 by Viktor E. Frankl
All rights reserved

Figures 1, 2, 3, 4, and 7 from "The Task of Education in an Age of
Meaninglessness," by Viktor E. Frankl, in Sidney S. Letter, ed., *New
Prospects for the Small Liberal Arts College* (New York: Teachers
College Press, 1968), used by permission of Teachers College Press.

 REGISTERED TRADEMARK—MARCA REGISTRADA

LIBRARY OF CONGRESS CATALOGING IN PUBLICATION DATA:

Frankl, Viktor Emil.
  The will to meaning.

  Includes indexes.
  1. Logotherapy.   I. Title.
RC489.L6F698   1988   616.89'16   88-12529

Printed in the United States of America

Without limiting the rights under copyright reserved above, no part
of this publication may be reproduced, stored in or introduced into
a retrieval system, or transmitted, in any form, or by any means
(electronic, mechanical, photocopying, recording, or otherwise),
without the prior written permission of both the copyright owner
and the above publisher of this book.

❦ ❦ ❦ IN MEMORIAM

GORDON W. ALLPORT

PREFACE

   ✿ ✿ ✿   THIS book is the outcome of a series of lectures I was invited to give during the 1966 summer session of Perkins School of Theology at Southern Methodist University in Dallas, Texas. The particular task assigned to me at that time was to explain the system that characterizes logotherapy. While it has often been pointed out by various authors that logotherapy, in contrast to the other schools of existential psychiatry, has developed a proper psychotherapeutic technique, it has scarcely been noticed that it also is the last psychotherapy that is conceptualized in a systematic way.[1]

Dealing with the *foundations* of the system, the chapters of this book set forth the basic assumptions and tenets underlying logotherapy. They form a chain of links interconnected with one another, in that logotherapy is based on the following three concepts: (1) the freedom of will; (2) the will to meaning; and (3) the meaning of life. (1) The freedom of will involves the issue of determinism versus pan-determinism. (2) The will to meaning is discussed as distinct from the concepts of the will to power and the will to pleasure as they are presented by

[1] Juan Battista Torello, in his introduction to the Italian edition of *Man's Search for Meaning*, has made this observation.

Adlerian and Freudian psychology, respectively. To be sure, the term, will to power, was coined by Nietzsche rather than Adler, and the term, will to pleasure—standing for Freud's pleasure principle—is my own and not Freud's. Moreover, the pleasure principle should be seen in the light of a broader concept, the homeostasis principle.[2] While criticizing both concepts, we shall have to elaborate on logotherapy's motivational theory. (3) The meaning of life relates to the issue of relativism versus subjectivism.

The *applications* of logotherapy discussed in this book are also threefold. First of all, logotherapy is applicable as a treatment of noogenic neuroses; second, logotherapy is a treatment of psychogenic neuroses, i.e., neuroses in the conventional sense of the word; and third, logotherapy is a treatment of somatogenic neuroses or, for that matter, somatogenic diseases in general. As we see, all the dimensions of a human being are reflected in this sequence of subject matters.

In the introductory chapter of this book, logotherapy is placed in perspective with other schools of psychotherapy, and, specifically, with existentialism in the field of psychotherapy. The last chapter deals with the dialogue between logotherapy and theology.

I have tried in this book to include the latest development of logotherapy with respect to both the formulation of the individual tenets and the material serving as an illustration. However, the attempt to offer a rounded picture of the whole system compels me to include some material which has been used in my previous books.[3]

[2] As to the reality principle, it serves the purposes of the pleasure principle in the same way as the latter serves the purposes of the homeostasis principle, and that is why there is no need to include it explicitly in our theory.

[3] See Viktor E. Frankl, *Man's Search for Meaning: An Introduction to Logotherapy*, Preface by Gordon W. Allport, Beacon Press, Boston,

What I term the existential vacuum constitutes a challenge to psychiatry today. Ever more patients complain of a feeling of emptiness and meaninglessness, which seems to me to derive from two facts. Unlike an animal, man is not told by instincts what he *must* do. And unlike man in former times, he is no longer told by traditions what he *should* do. Often he does not even know what he basically wishes to do. Instead, either he wishes to do what other people do (conformism), or he does what other people wish him to do (totalitarianism).

I hope that I shall be successful in conveying to the reader my conviction that, despite the crumbling of traditions, life holds a meaning for each and every individual, and even more, it retains this meaning literally to his last breath. And the psychiatrist can show his patient that life never ceases to have a meaning. To be sure, he cannot show his patient *what* the meaning is, but he may well show him that *there is* a meaning, and that life retains it: that it remains meaningful, under any conditions. As logotherapy teaches, even the tragic and negative aspects of life, such as unavoidable suffering, can be turned into a human achievement by the attitude which a man adopts toward his predicament. In contrast to most of the existentialist schools of thought, logotherapy is in no way pessimistic; but it is realistic in that it faces the tragic triad of human existence: pain, death, and guilt. Logotherapy may justly be called optimistic, because it shows the patient how to transform despair into triumph.

In an age such as ours, in which traditions are on the wane, psychiatry must see its principal assignment in equipping man

1962 (Paperback edition: Washington Square Press, New York, 1963); *The Doctor and the Soul: An Introduction to Logotherapy,* revised edition, Alfred A. Knopf, New York, 1965 (paperback edition: Bantam Books, New York, 1967); *Psychotherapy and Existentialism, Selected Papers on Logotherapy,* Washington Square Press, New York, 1967 (paperback edition: Clarion Books, 1968).

with the ability to find meaning. In an age in which the Ten Commandments seem to many people to have lost their unconditional validity, man must learn to listen to the ten thousand commandments implied in the ten thousand situations of which his life consists. In this respect I hope the reader will find that logotherapy speaks to the needs of the hour.

VIKTOR E. FRANKL, M.D., Ph.D.

Vienna, Austria

CONTENTS

INTRODUCTION

THE SITUATION OF PSYCHO-
THERAPY AND THE POSITION
OF LOGOTHERAPY

❦ ❦ ❦ THE present situation of psychotherapy is characterized by the rise of existential psychiatry. In fact, one could speak of an inoculation of existentialism in psychiatry as a major contemporary trend. But in speaking of existentialism we must bear in mind that there are as many existentialisms as there are existentialists. Moreover, not only has each existentialist molded his own version of the philosophy, but also each uses the nomenclature differently from the way others use it. For example, such terms as existence and *Dasein* have meanings deviating from each other in the writings of Jaspers and Heidegger.

Nonetheless, the individual authors in the field of existential psychiatry have something in common—a common denominator. It is the phrase so often used by these authors—and all too often misused by them: "being in the world." One gets the impression that many of these authors think it is a sufficient credential to be considered a true existentialist if they apply the phrase "being in the world" time and again. I doubt that this is a sufficient ground for calling oneself an existentialist, particularly since, as could easily be demonstrated, in most cases Heidegger's concept of being in the world is misconceived in the direction of mere subjectivism—as though "the world" in which a human being "is" were nothing but a self-expression of the being himself. I venture to criticize this widespread misconception only because, as it happens, I once had an opportunity to discuss it in personal conversation with Martin Heidegger himself, and found that he agreed with me.

Misunderstandings in the field of existentialism may be understood easily. The terminology is sometimes esoteric, to say the least. About thirty years ago, I had to give a public lecture on psychiatry and existentialism in Vienna. I confronted my audience with two quotations and told them that one was taken from Heidegger's writings while the other was part of a conversation that I had had with a schizophrenic patient institutionalized in Vienna's state hospital where I was then on the staff. And then I invited my audience to vote on which one was whose. Believe it or not, an overwhelming majority thought that the passage quoted from Heidegger was the utterance of a schizophrenic patient and vice versa. However, we must not draw rash conclusions from the result of this experiment. By no means does it speak against the greatness of Heidegger—and let us take it for granted that he is as great as many experts believe. Rather it speaks against the capacity of everyday language to express thoughts and feelings hitherto unknown—be they revolutionary ideas created by a great philosopher, or strange feelings experienced by a schizophrenic individual. What unites them is a crisis of expression, as it were, and elsewhere I have shown that something analogous holds for the modern artist (see my book, *Psychotherapy and Existentialism, Selected Papers on Logotherapy*, Washington Square Press, New York, 1967, the chapter on "Psychotherapy, Art and Religion").

As to the position of the method I have called logotherapy, which is the subject of this book, most authors agree that it falls under the category of existential psychiatry.[1] In fact, as early as the thirties I coined the word *Existenzanalyse* as an alternative name for logotherapy, which I had coined in the twenties. Later on, when American authors started publishing in the field of logotherapy they introduced the term "existential analysis" as a translation of *Existenzanalyse*. Unfortunately, other authors did the same with the word *Daseinsanalyse*—a term which, in the forties, had been selected by the late Ludwig Binswanger, the great Swiss psychiatrist, to denote his own teachings. Since then existential analysis has become quite an ambiguous word. In order not to add to the confusion which had been aroused by this state of affairs, I decided to refrain more and more from using the term existential analysis in my publications in English. Often I speak of logotherapy even in a context where no therapy in the strict sense of the word is involved. What I call medical ministry, for example, forms an important aspect of the practice of logotherapy but it is indicated precisely in those cases where actual therapy is impossible because the patient is confronted with an incurable disease. Yet, in the widest possible sense, logotherapy *is* treat-

[1] Pertinent statements may be found in the following: Gordon W. Allport, in Viktor E. Frankl, *Man's Search for Meaning: An Introduction to Logotherapy*, Washington Square Press, New York, 1963; Aaron J. Ungersma, *The Search for Meaning: A New Approach to Psychotherapy and Pastoral Psychology*, The Westminster Press, Philadelphia, 1961; Donald F. Tweedie, *Logotherapy and the Christian Faith: An Evaluation of Frankl's Existential Approach to Psychotherapy*, Baker Book House, Grand Rapids, Michigan, 1965; Robert C. Leslie, *Jesus and Logotherapy: The Ministry of Jesus as Interpreted Through the Psychotherapy of Viktor Frankl*, Abingdon Press, New York, 1965; Godfryd Kaczanowski, in Arthur Burton, *Modern Psychotherapeutic Practice: Innovations in Technique*, Science and Behavior Books, Palo Alto, California, 1965; James C. Crumbaugh, "The Application of Logotherapy," *Journal of Existentialism* 5: 403-412, 1965; Joseph Lyons, "Existential Psychotherapy: Fact, Hope, Fiction," *Journal of Abnormal and Social Psychology* 62: 242-249, 1961; and Lawrence A. Pervin, "Existentialism, Psychology, and Psychotherapy," *American Psychologist* 15: 305-309, 1960.

ment even then—it is treatment of the patient's attitude toward his unchangeable fate.

Logotherapy has not only been subsumed under the heading of existential psychiatry but has also been acclaimed, within this province, as the only school which has succeeded in developing what one might be justified in calling a technique.[2] However, this is not to say that we logotherapists overrate the importance of techniques. One has long ago come to realize that what matters in therapy is not techniques but rather the human relations between doctor and patient, or the personal and existential encounter.

A purely technological approach to psychotherapy may block its therapeutic effect. Some time ago I was invited to lecture at an American university before a team of psychiatrists who had been assigned the care of the evacuees after a hurricane. I not only accepted this invitation but even selected the title, "Techniques and Dynamics of Survival," a title that obviously pleased the sponsors of my lecture. But when I started this lecture I frankly told them that as long as we actually interpret our task merely in terms of techniques and dynamics we have missed the point—and we have missed the hearts of those to whom we wish to offer mental first aid. Approaching human beings merely in terms of techniques necessarily implies manipulating them, and approaching them merely in terms of dynamics implies reifying them, making human beings into mere things. And these human beings immediately feel and notice the manipulative quality of our approach and our tendency to reify them. I would say, reification has become the original sin of psychotherapy. But a human being is no thing. This *no-thingness, rather than nothingness, is the lesson to learn from existentialism.*

[2] This at least is the contention of such authors as Ungersma, Tweedie, Leslie, Kaczanowski, Lyons, and Crumbaugh.

When, on the occasion of another lecture tour, I was asked to address the prisoners at San Quentin I was assured, afterward, that in a way it was the first time they really felt understood. What I had done was nothing so extraordinary. I had simply taken them as human beings and not mistaken them for mechanisms to repair. I had interpreted them in the same way they had interpreted themselves all along, that is to say, as free and responsible. I had not offered them a cheap escape from guilt feelings by conceiving of them as victims of biological, psychological, or sociological conditioning processes. Nor had I taken them as helpless pawns on the battleground of id, ego, and superego. I had not provided them with an alibi. Guilt had not been taken away from them. I had not explained it away. I had taken them as peers. They learned that it was a prerogative of man to become guilty—and his responsibility to overcome guilt.

What did I implement when addressing the prisoners at San Quentin if not phenomenology in the truest sense? In fact, phenomenology is an attempt to describe the way in which man understands himself, in which he interprets his own existence, far from preconceived patterns of interpretation and explanation such as are furnished by psychodynamic or socio-economic hypotheses. In adopting the phenomenological methodology, logotherapy, as Paul Polak[3] once put it, tries to couch man's unbiased self-understanding in scientific terms.

Let me again take up the issue of technique versus encounter. Psychotherapy is more than mere technique in that it is art, and it goes beyond pure science in that it is wisdom. But even wisdom is not the last word. In a concentration camp I once saw the body of a woman who had committed suicide. Among her effects there was a scrap of paper on which she had writ-

[3] Paul Polak, "Fra... Journal of Psychotherapy 3: 517

7

ten the words: "More powerful than fate is the courage that bears it." Despite this motto she had taken her life. Wisdom is lacking without the human touch.

Recently, I received a telephone call at three in the morning from a lady who told me that she was determined to commit suicide but was curious to know what I would say about it. I replied with all the arguments against this resolution and for survival, and I talked to her for thirty minutes—until she finally gave her word that she would not take her life but rather come to see me in the hospital. But when she visited me there it turned out that not one of all the arguments I offered had impressed her. The only reason she had decided not to commit suicide was the fact that, rather than growing angry because of having been disturbed in my sleep in the middle of the night, I had patiently listened to her and talked with her for half an hour, and a world—she found—in which this can happen, must be a world worth living in.

As far as psychotherapy is concerned, it is mainly to the credit of the late Ludwig Binswanger that the human being has been reinstalled and reinstated in his humanness. And more and more the I-Thou relation can be regarded as the heart of the matter. Yet even beyond this is another dimension still to be entered. The encounter between I and Thou cannot be the whole truth, the whole story. The essentially self-transcendent quality of human existence renders man *a being reaching out beyond himself*. Therefore, if Martin Buber, along with Ferdinand Ebner, interprets human existence basically in terms of a dialogue between I and Thou, we must recognize that this dialogue defeats itself unless I and Thou transcend themselves to refer to a meaning outside themselves.

Insofar as psychotherapy—rather than merely being psychological engineering and technology—is based on encounter, what encounter one another are not two monads but rather human beings, of which one confronts the other with logos, that is, the meaning of being.

By placing an emphasis on an encounter I to Thou, *Daseinsanalyse* has made the partners of such an encounter truly listen to one another and thus freed them from their ontological deafness, one could say. But we still have to free them from their ontological blindness, we still have to make the meaning of being shine forth. This is the step taken by logotherapy. Logotherapy goes beyond *Daseinsanalyse* or (to adopt the translation by Jordan M. Scher) ontoanalysis, in that it is not only concerned with ontos, or being, but also with logos, or meaning. This may well account for the fact that logotherapy is more than mere analysis; it is, as the very name indicates, therapy. In a personal conversation Ludwig Binswanger once told me that he felt that, compared with ontoanalysis, logotherapy was more activistic, and even more, that logotherapy could lend itself as the therapeutic supplement to ontoanalysis.

By way of a deliberate oversimplification, one could define logotherapy by the literal translation as healing through meaning (Joseph B. Fabry).[4] Of course we must keep in mind that logotherapy, far from being a panacea, is indicated in certain cases and contraindicated in other ones. As will be seen in the second section of this volume, when the applications of logotherapy will be dealt with, it is applicable in cases of neurosis, to begin with. Here another distinction between logotherapy and ontoanalysis becomes apparent. One could epitomize Binswanger's contribution to psychiatry in terms of a better understanding of psychosis, more specifically, the particular and peculiar mode of psychotic being-in-the-world. In contra-

[4] Joseph B. Fabry, *The Pursuit of Meaning: Logotherapy Applied to Life*, Preface by Viktor E. Frankl, Beacon Press, Boston, 1968.

distinction to ontoanalysis, logotherapy does not aim at a better understanding of psychosis but rather at a shorter treatment of neurosis. Another oversimplification, to be sure.

In this context, those authors deserve to be mentioned who contend that Binswanger's work boils down to an application of Heideggerian concepts to psychiatry, while logotherapy is the result of an application of Max Scheler's concepts to psychotherapy.

Now—after speaking of Scheler and Heidegger and the influence of their philosophies on logotherapy—what about Freud and Adler? Is logotherapy less indebted to them? By no means. As a matter of fact, in the first paragraph of the first book of mine the reader finds an expression of this indebtedness when I invoke the analogy of a dwarf who, standing on the shoulders of a giant, sees a bit farther than the giant himself. After all, psychoanalysis is, and will remain forever, the indispensable foundation of every psychotherapy, including any future schools. However, it will also have to share the fate of a foundation, that is to say, it will become invisible to the extent to which the proper building is erected on it.

Freud was too much of a genius not to be aware of the fact that he had limited his research to the foundations, to the deeper layers, to the lower dimensions of human existence. In a letter to Ludwig Binswanger he said himself: "I have always confined myself to the ground floor and basement of the edifice" called man.[5]

In a book review[6] Freud once expressed his conviction that reverence before a great master is a good thing, but should be surpassed and exceeded by our reverence before facts. Let us

[5] Ludwig Binswanger, *Reminiscences of a Friendship,* Grune & Stratton, New York, 1957, p. 96.

[6] Sigmund Freud, "Über Forel: Der Hypnotismus, seine Bedeutung und seine Handhabung," *Wiener medizinische Wochenschrift* 34: 1098, 1889.

now try to reinterpret and reevaluate Freud's psychoanalysis in the light of those facts which only came to the fore after Freud had died.

Such a reinterpretation of psychoanalysis deviates from Freud's own self-interpretation. Columbus believed that he had found a new way to India, when what he had discovered was a new continent. There is also a difference between what Freud believed and what he achieved. Freud believed that man could be explained by a mechanistic theory and that his psyche could be cured by means of techniques. But what he achieved was something different, something still tenable, provided that we reevaluate it in the light of existential facts.

According to a statement once made by Sigmund Freud, psychoanalysis rests on the recognition of two concepts, repression as the cause of neurosis and transference as its cure. Whoever believes in the importance of these two concepts may justifiably regard and call himself a psychoanalyst.

Repression is counteracted by growing awareness. Repressed material should be made conscious. Or, as Freud put it, where id had been, ego should become. Freed from the mechanistic ideology of the nineteenth century, seen in the light of the existentialist philosophy of the twentieth century, one could say that psychoanalysis promotes self-understanding in man.

Similarly, the concept of transference can be refined and purged. The Adlerian psychologist Rudolf Dreikurs once pointed to the manipulative quality inherent in the Freudian concept of transference.[7] Freed from its manipulative quality, transference could be understood as a vehicle of that human and personal encounter which is based on the I-Thou relation. As a matter of fact, if self-understanding is to be reached, it has to be mediated by encounter. In other words, Freud's state-

[7] Rudolf Dreikurs, "The Current Dilemma in Psychotherapy," *Journal of Existential Psychiatry* 1: 187-206, 1960.

ment, where id is, ego should be, could be enlarged: Where id is, ego should be; *but the ego can become an ego only through a Thou.*

As to that material which had fallen prey to repression, Freud believed that it was sex. In fact, in his time, sex was repressed even on a mass level. This was a consequence of puritanism, and this puritanism was predominant in Anglo-Saxon countries. Small wonder that it was these countries that proved to be most receptive to psychoanalysis—and resistant to those schools of psychotherapy that went beyond Freud.

To identify psychoanalysis with psychology or psychiatry would be as great a mistake as to identify dialectical materialism with sociology. Both Freudianism and Marxism are single approaches to sciences rather than the sciences themselves. To be sure, indoctrination—Western as well as Eastern style—may blur the difference between what is sect and what is science.

In a way, however, psychoanalysis is irreplaceable. And the place still reserved to Freud as far as the history of psychotherapy is concerned reminds me of a story they tell at the oldest synagogue of the world, Prague's medieval Alt Neu Synagogue. When the guide there shows you the interior, he tells you that the seat once occupied by the famous Rabbi Loew has never been taken over by any of his followers; another seat has been set up for them, because Rabbi Loew could never be replaced, no one could match him. For centuries no one was allowed to sit down on his seat. The chair of Freud should also be kept empty.

PART ONE

✼ ✼ ✼

FOUNDATIONS OF
LOGOTHERAPY

METACLINICAL IMPLICATIONS

OF PSYCHOTHERAPY

⚜ ⚜ ⚜ THE metaclinical implications of psychotherapy refer mainly to its concept of man and philosophy of life. There is no psychotherapy without a theory of man and a philosophy of life underlying it. Wittingly or unwittingly, psychotherapy is based on them. In this respect psychoanalysis is no exception. Paul Schilder called psychoanalysis a *Weltanschauung*, and only recently F. Gordon Pleune said that "the psychoanalytic practitioner is a moralist first and foremost" and "influences people in regard to their moral and ethical conduct."[1]

Thus the issue cannot be whether or not psychotherapy is based on a *Weltanschauung* but rather, whether the *Weltanschauung* underlying it is right or wrong. Right or wrong, however, in this context means whether or not the humanness of man is preserved in a given philosophy and theory. The human quality of a human being is disregarded and neglected, for example, by those psychologists who adhere to either "the

---

[1] F. Gordon Pleune, "All Dis-Ease Is Not Disease: A Consideration of Psycho-Analysis, Psychotherapy, and Psycho-Social Engineering," *International Journal of Psycho-Analysis* 46: 358, 1965. Quoted from *Digest of Neurology and Psychiatry* 34: 148, 1966.

machine model" or "the rat model," as Gordon W. Allport[2] termed them. As to the first, I deem it to be a remarkable fact that man, as long as he regarded himself as a creature, interpreted his existence in the image of God, his creator; but as soon as he started considering himself as a creator, began to interpret his existence merely in the image of his own creation, the machine.

Logotherapy's concept of man is based on three pillars, the freedom of will, the will to meaning, and the meaning of life. The first of them, the freedom of will, is opposed to a principle that characterizes most current approaches to man, namely, determinism. Really, however, it is only opposed to what I am used to calling pan-determinism, because speaking of the freedom of will does not in any way imply any *a priori* indeterminism. After all, the freedom of will means the freedom of human will, and human will is the will of a finite being. Man's freedom is no freedom from conditions but rather freedom to take a stand on whatever conditions might confront him.

During an interview, Huston C. Smith of Harvard (then at MIT) asked me whether I as a professor of neurology and psychiatry would not concede that man is subject to conditions and determinants. I answered that as a neurologist and psychiatrist, of course, I am fully aware of the extent to which man is not at all free from conditions, be they biological, psychological, or sociological. But I added that along with being a professor in two fields (neurology and psychiatry) I am a survivor of four camps (that is, concentration camps), and as such I also bear witness to the unexpected extent to which man is, and always remains, capable of resisting and braving even the worst conditions. To detach oneself from even the worst

[2] Gordon W. Allport, *Personality and Social Encounter*, Beacon Press, Boston, 1960.

conditions is a uniquely human capability. However, this unique capacity of man to detach himself from any situations he might have to face is manifested not only through heroism, as was the case in the concentration camps, but also through humor. Humor, too, is a uniquely human capacity. And we need not feel ashamed of this fact. Humor is said even to be a divine attribute. In three psalms God is referred to as a "laughing" one.

Humor and heroism refer us to the uniquely human capacity of *self-detachment*. By virtue of this capacity man is capable of detaching himself not only from a situation but also from himself. He is capable of choosing his attitude toward himself. By so doing he really takes a stand toward his own somatic and psychic conditions and determinants. Understandably this is a crucial issue for psychotherapy and psychiatry, education and religion. For, seen in this light, a person is free to shape his own character, and man is responsible for what he may have made out of himself. What matters is not the features of our character or the drives and instincts per se, but rather the stand we take toward them. And the capacity to take such a stand is what makes us human beings.

Taking a stand toward somatic and psychic phenomena implies rising above their level and opening a new dimension, the dimension of noetic phenomena, or the noological dimension —in contradistinction to the biological and psychological ones. It is that dimension in which the uniquely human phenomena are located.

It could be defined as the spiritual dimension as well. However, since in English "spiritual" has a religious connotation, this term must be avoided as much as possible. For what we understand by the noological dimension is the anthropological rather than the theological dimension. This also holds for "logos" in the context with "logotherapy." In addition to meaning "meaning," "logos" here means "spirit"—but again without any primarily religious connotation. Here "logos" means the humanness of the human being—plus the meaning of being human!

Man passes the noological dimension whenever he is reflecting upon himself—or, if need be, rejecting himself; whenever he is making himself an object—or making objections to himself; whenever he displays his being conscious of himself—or whenever he exhibits his being conscientious. In fact, being conscientious presupposes the uniquely human capacity to rise above oneself, to judge and evaluate one's own deeds in moral and ethical terms.

Of course one may rob a uniquely human phenomenon such as conscience of its humanness. One may conceive of conscience merely in terms of the result of conditioning processes. But actually such an interpretation is appropriate and adequate only, for example, in the case of a dog which has wet the carpet and slinks under the couch with its tail between its legs. Does this dog actually manifest conscience? I rather think that it manifests the fearful expectation of punishment—which might well be the result of conditioning processes.

Reducing conscience to the mere result of conditioning processes is but one instance of reductionism. I would define reductionism as a pseudoscientific approach which disregards and ignores the humanness of phenomena by making them into mere epiphenomena, more specifically, by reducing them to subhuman phenomena. In fact, one could define reductionism as *sub-humanism*.

To give an example, let me take up two phenomena which perhaps are the most human ones, love and conscience. These two are the most striking manifestations of another uniquely human capacity, the capacity of *self-transcendence*. Man transcends himself either toward another human being or toward meaning. Love, I would say, is that capacity which enables him to grasp the other human being in his very uniqueness. Conscience is that capacity which empowers him to seize the meaning of a situation in its very uniqueness, and in the final analysis meaning is something unique. So is each and every person. Ultimately every person is irreplaceable, and if for no other person he is so for him by whom he is loved.

Because of the uniqueness of the intentional referents of love and conscience, both are intuitive capacities. However, along with the denominator of uniqueness common to the intentional referents, there is a difference between them. The uniqueness envisaged by love refers to the unique possibilities the loved person may have. On the other hand, the uniqueness envisaged by conscience refers to a unique necessity, to a unique need one may have to meet.

Now, reductionism is liable to interpret love as a mere sublimation of sex, and conscience merely in terms of the superego. It is my contention that actually love could not be just the result of the sublimation of sex because, whenever sublimation takes place, love has been the precondition all along. I would say that only to the extent to which an I is lovingly directed toward a Thou—only to this extent is the ego also capable of integrating the id, of integrating the sexuality into the personality.

And conscience cannot be merely the superego—for the simple reason that conscience is assigned if need be to oppose precisely those conventions and standards, traditions and values which are transmitted by the superego. Thus, if conscience may have, in a given case, the function of contradicting the superego, it certainly cannot be identical with the superego. Reducing conscience to the superego and deducing love from the id are both doomed to failure.

Let us ask what may have caused reductionism. To answer

this question we must consider the effects of scientific special-ization. We are living in an age of specialists, and this takes its toll. I would define *a specialist* as a man who *no longer sees the forest of truth for the trees of facts*. To choose one example, in the field of schizophrenia, we are confronted with a lot of findings furnished by biochemistry. We are also facing a vast literature on the hypothetical psychodynamics underlying schizophrenia. And another literature is concerned with the uniquely schizophrenic mode of being in the world. However, I deem that he who contends that he knows what schizophrenia really is is deceiving you, or at best himself.

The pictures by which the individual sciences depict reality have become so disparate, so different from each other, that it has become more and more difficult to obtain a fusion of the different pictures. The difference between pictures need not constitute a loss, but may well form a gain in knowledge. In the case of stereoscopic vision, it is the very difference between the right and the left picture that makes for the acquisition of a whole dimension, that is, the three-dimensional space over against the two-dimensional plane. To be sure, there is a precon-dition. The retinas must be capable of arriving at a fusion of the different pictures!

What holds for vision is also true of cognition. The chal-lenge is how to attain, how to maintain, and how to restore a unified concept of man in the face of the scattered data, facts, and findings supplied by a compartmentalized science of man.

But we cannot draw back the wheel of history. Society cannot do without specialists. Too much of the style of re-search has become characterized by teamwork, and in the framework of teamwork the specialist is indispensable.

But does the danger really lie in the lack of universality? Doesn't it rather lurk in the pretense of totality? What is dangerous is the attempt of a man who is an expert, say, in the field of biology, to understand and explain human beings exclusively in terms of biology. The same is true of psychology and sociology as well. At the moment at which totality is claimed, biology becomes biologism, psychology becomes psychologism, and sociology becomes sociologism. In other words, at that moment science is turned into ideology. What we have to deplore, I would say, is not that *scientists are specializing* but that the *specialists are generalizing*. We are familiar with that type called *terrible simplificateurs*. Now we become acquainted with a type I would like to call *terrible généralisateurs*. I mean those who cannot resist the temptation to make overgeneralized statements on the grounds of limited findings.

I once came across a quotation defining man as "nothing but a complex biochemical mechanism powered by a combustion system which energizes computors with prodigious storage facilities for retaining encoded information." Now, as a neurologist, I stand for the justification of using the computor as a model, say, for the activity of the central nervous system. It is perfectly legitimate to use such an analogy. Thus, in a certain sense the statement is valid: man is a computor. However, at the same time he also is infinitely more than a computor. The statement is erroneous only insofar as man is defined as "nothing but" a computor.

Today nihilism no longer unmasks itself by speaking of "nothingness." Today nihilism is masked by speaking of the "nothing-but-ness" of man. Reductionism has become the mask of nihilism.

How should we cope with this state of affairs? How is it possible to preserve the humanness of man in the face of reductionism? In the final analysis, how is it possible to preserve the oneness of man in the face of the pluralism of sciences, when the pluralism of sciences is the nourishing soil on which reductionism is flourishing?

Nicolai Hartmann and Max Scheler, perhaps more than anyone else, have tried to solve the problem confronting us. Hartmann's ontology and Scheler's anthropology are attempts to allot to each science a province of limited validity. Hartmann distinguished various strata such as the bodily and mental ones plus a spiritual apex. Here again spiritual is meant without a religious connotation, but rather in the sense of noological. Hartmann sees the stratification of human existence as a hierarchical structure. By contrast, Scheler's anthropology uses the image of layers (*Schichten*) rather than strata (*Stufen*), thereby distinguishing the more or less peripheral biological and psychological layers from the central personal one—the spiritual axis.

Certainly both Hartmann and Scheler have done justice to the ontological differences between body, mind, and spirit by conceiving of them in terms of qualitative rather than merely quantitative differences. However, they do not take into sufficient account what is opposed to the ontological differences, namely, what I would like to call the anthropological unity on the other hand. Or, as Thomas Aquinas put it, man is a *"unitas multiplex."* Art has been defined as unity in diversity. I would define man as unity in spite of multiplicity!

Conceiving of man in terms of bodily, mental, and spiritual strata or layers means dealing with him as if his somatic, psychic, and noetic modes of being could be separated from each other.

I myself have tried simultaneously to do justice to the ontological differences and the anthropological unity by what I have called dimensional anthropology and ontology. This approach makes use of the geometrical concept of dimensions as an analogy for qualitative differences which do not destroy the unity of a structure.

Dimensional ontology as I have propounded it, rests on two laws. The first law of dimensional ontology reads: One and the same phenomenon projected out of its own dimension into different dimensions lower than its own is depicted in such a way that the individual pictures contradict one another.

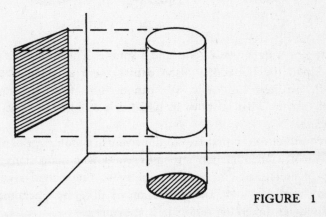

FIGURE 1

Imagine a cylinder, say, a cup. Projected out of its three-dimensional space into the horizontal and vertical two-dimensional planes, it yields in the first case a circle and in the second one a rectangle. These pictures contradict one another. What is even more important, the cup is an open vessel in contrast to the circle and the rectangle which are closed figures. Another contradiction!

Now let us proceed to the second law of dimensional ontology which reads: Different phenomena projected out of their own dimension into one dimension lower than their own are depicted in such a manner that the pictures are ambiguous.

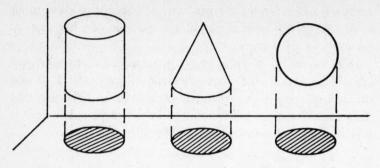

FIGURE 2

Imagine a cylinder, a cone, and a sphere. The shadows they cast upon the horizontal plane depict them as three circles which are interchangeable. We cannot infer from a shadow what casts it, what is above it, whether a cylinder, a cone, or a sphere.

According to the first law of dimensional ontology, the projection of a phenomenon into different lower dimensions results in inconsistencies, and according to the second law of dimensional ontology, the projection of different phenomena into a lower dimension results in isomorphies.

Now how should we apply these images to anthropology and ontology? Once we have projected man into the biological and psychological dimensions we also obtain contradictory results. For in the one case a biological organism is the result; in the other one, a psychological mechanism. But, however the bodily and mental aspects of human existence might contradict one another, seen in the light of dimensional anthropology this contradiction no longer contradicts the oneness of man. Or does the contradiction between a circle and a rectangle contradict the fact that both result from a projection of the same cylinder?

Dimensional ontology is far from solving the mind-body problem. But it does explain why the mind-body problem cannot be solved. Of necessity the unity of man—a unity in spite of the multiplicity of body and mind—cannot be found in the biological or psychological but must be sought in that noological dimension out of which man is projected in the first place.[3]

However, alongside the problem of mind versus body, there is the problem of determinism, the problem of freedom of choice. But this problem, too, may well be approached along the lines of dimensional anthropology. The openness of a cup necessarily disappears in the horizontal and vertical dimensions. Well, man, too, projected into a dimension lower than his own seems to be a closed system, be it of physiological reflexes or psychological reactions and responses to stimuli. Those motivational theories, e.g., which still adhere to the homeostasis principle, deal with man as with a closed system. This, however, means disregarding and neglecting that essential openness of human existence which has been evidenced by Max Scheler, Adolf Portmann, and Arnold Gehlen. Particularly the biologist Portmann and the sociologist Gehlen have shown us that man is open to the world. Because of the self-transcendent quality of human existence, I would say, being human always means

[3] Before answering Kant's and the psalmist's question, "What is man?" we must turn it into the question, "Where is man?" In which dimension is the humanness of a human being to be found? Once we embark on reductionism by stating a priori that man is nothing but an animal, we cannot discover anything else. This procedure compares to that of the rabbi who, as a joke has it, was consulted by two men, one of whom contended that his neighbor's cat had stolen and eaten five pounds of butter. The owner of the cat denied that it had ever cared for butter. The rabbi weighed the cat and, behold, its weight was exactly five pounds. "Now I have the butter," the rabbi mused, "but where is the cat?" Well, where then is man once our investigation is confined to the biological dimension and restricted to a biologistic projection?

being directed and pointing to something or someone other than itself.

All this disappears in the biological and psychological dimensions. But in the light of dimensional anthropology we can at least understand why this must happen. Now the apparent closedness of man in the biological and psychological dimensions no longer contradicts the humanness of man. Closedness in the lower dimensions is very compatible with openness in a higher one, be it the openness of a cylindrical cup, or that of a human being.

Now it may also have become understandable why sound findings of research in the lower dimensions, however they may neglect the humanness of man, need not contradict it. This is equally true of approaches as distinct as Watsonian behaviorism, Pavlovian reflexology, Freudian psychoanalysis, and Adlerian psychology. They are not nullified by logotherapy but rather overarched by it. They are seen in the light of a higher dimension—or, as the Norwegian psychotherapist Bjarne Kvilhaug[4] put it with special reference to learning theory and behavior therapy, the findings of these schools are reinterpreted and reevaluated by logotherapy—and rehumanized by it.

In this context a warning remark is necessary. Speaking of higher as opposed to lower dimensions does not imply a value judgment. A "higher" dimension just means a more inclusive and encompassing dimension.[5]

This is a crucial issue in anthropology. It implies no more

---

[4] Bjarne Kvilhaug, Paper read before Austrian Medical Society of Psychotherapy on July 18, 1963.

[5] I well remember how insistent and inquisitive the late Paul Tillich was in the question-and-answer period following my presentation of dimensional ontology at a faculty luncheon of Harvard's Divinity School. He was satisfied only after I had defined the higher dimension as a more inclusive one.

nor less than the recognition that man, by having become a human being, in no way ceases to remain an animal, any more than an airplane ceases to be capable of moving around the ground of the airport.

As I pointed out in the Introduction, Freud was too great not to be aware that he had always confined himself "to the ground floor and basement of the edifice," in other words, that he had confined himself to a lower, the psychological, dimension. He became a victim of reductionism only when he continued his letter to Ludwig Binswanger by declaring that he had "already found a place for religion, by putting it under the category of the neurosis of mankind." Even a genius cannot completely resist his *Zeitgeist*, the spirit of his era.

Now let us see how the second law of dimensional ontology may be applied to man. Well, we need only replace the three ambiguous circles by neuroses, because neuroses, too, are ambiguous. A neurosis may be psychogenic, i.e., a neurosis in the conventional sense. Moreover, my own research has taught me that there are also somatogenic neuroses. There are cases of agoraphobia, for example, which are caused by hyperthyroidism. And, last but not least, there are noogenic neuroses, as I have called them. They originate in spiritual problems, in moral conflicts, or in that conflict between a true conscience and the mere superego which I referred to at the outset of this chapter. Most important, however, are those noogenic neuroses which result from the frustration of the will to meaning, from what I have called existential frustration, or from the existential vacuum to which a chapter of its own is devoted in this book.

To the degree, then, to which the etiology of neuroses is multidimensional, their symptomatology becomes ambiguous. And, as we could not infer from a circular shadow whether a cylinder, a cone, or a sphere stands above it, we cannot conclude whether hyperthyroidism, castration fear, or an existential vacuum stands behind a neurosis. At least we cannot do so as long as we confine ourselves to the psychological dimension.

Pathology is ambiguous in that, in a given case, we still have to search for the logos of pathos, for the meaning of suffering. And the meaning of suffering need not dwell in the same dimension as the symptomatology but may well hide in another dimension. The multidimensional etiology of neuroses requires what I would like to call a dimensional diagnosis.

What holds for diagnosis is true of therapy as well. Therapy too, must be multidimensionally oriented. There is no *a priori* objection against "shots and shocks." In cases of what is called in psychiatry an endogenous depression it is perfectly legitimate and justified to use drugs and, in severe cases, even to apply electroconvulsive treatment. As it happens it was I who developed the first tranquilizing drug on the Continent, before the Anglo-Saxon march to Miltown was started. In exceptional cases I have ordered lobotomies and in some cases even performed such brain surgery myself. It goes without saying that all this does not obviate the need for simultaneous psychotherapy—and logotherapy—since even in such cases we are not merely treating diseases but dealing with human beings.

Thus I cannot share the apprehension of those speakers who at an international meeting said that they were afraid psychiatry might become mechanized and patients might feel depersonalized if we embark on pharmacotherapy. In the Department of Neurology at the Poliklinik Hospital of Vienna, my staff makes use of drugs and, if need be, even of shocks, and yet no violence is done to the human dignity of the patients. On the other hand, I know of many depth psychologists who would abhor prescribing a drug, not to mention applying a shock, but by their very concept of man, by their mechanistic approach to man, they do violate the human dignity of their patients. That is why I feel that it is important to make the concept of man by which we approach our patients conscious to ourselves, and to make the meta-clinical implications of psychotherapy explicit.

What matters is never a technique per se but rather the spirit in which the technique is used. This holds not only for drugs and electroshocks, but for Freudian psychoanalysis, for Adlerian psychology, and for logotherapy as well.

Now let us come back to the second law of dimensional ontology and, for a change, substitute a historic for the geometric figures. More specifically, let us assume that the first circular shadow stands for a case of schizophrenia with auditory hallucinations, while the second circular shadow stands for Joan of Arc. There is no doubt that from the psychiatric point of view, the saint would have had to be diagnosed as a case of schizophrenia; and as long as we confine ourselves to the psychiatric frame of reference, Joan of Arc is "nothing but" a schizophrenic. What she is beyond a schizophrenic is not perceptible within the psychiatric dimension. As soon as we follow her into the noological dimension and observe her theological and historical importance, it turns out that Joan of Arc is more than a schizophrenic. The fact of her being a schizophrenic in the dimension of psychiatry does not in the least detract from her significance in other dimensions. And vice versa. Even if we took it for granted that she was a saint, this would not change the fact that she was also a schizophrenic.

A psychiatrist should confine himself to the dimension of psychiatry rather than conclude from a psychiatric phenomenon whether it is nothing but, or more than, a psychiatric phenomenon. Confining himself to the dimension of psychiatry, however, implies projecting a given phenomenon into the dimension of psychiatry. This is perfectly legitimate as long as the psychiatrist is aware of what he does. Even more, projections are not only legitimate but also obligatory in science. Science cannot cope with reality in its multidimensionality but must deal with reality as if reality were unidimensional. However, a scientist should remain aware of what he does, if for no other reason than to avoid the pitfalls of reductionism.

Another example of ambiguity of projections occurred years ago in the block in which I live in Vienna. The owner of a tobacco shop was assaulted by a hoodlum and in the emergency she cried out for Franz, her husband. A curtain divided the shop, and the hoodlum expected Franz to come out from behind the curtain at any moment. He fled and was caught. A sequence of natural events, is it not? But actually, Franz had died two weeks earlier, and his wife had sent a prayer to Heaven imploring her husband to intervene with God for her rescue. Well, it is entirely up to each of us how we wish to interpret this sequence of natural facts, whether in terms of a misunderstanding on the part of the hoodlum, that is to say, psychologically, or in terms of Heaven having accepted a prayer. I for one am convinced that if there is such a thing as Heaven, and if Heaven ever accepts a prayer, it will hide this behind a sequence of natural facts.

SELF-TRANSCENDENCE

AS A HUMAN PHENOMENON

ᵞᵉ ᵞᵉ ᵞᵉ IN the last chapter I said that man is open to the world. He is so in contrast to animals, which are not open to the world (*Welt*) but rather bound to an environment (*Umwelt*) which is specific to their species. The environment contains what is of appeal to the instinctual makeup of a species. By contrast it is a characteristic constituent of human existence to break through the barriers of the environment of the species *homo sapiens*. Man is reaching out for, and actually reaching, finally attaining, the world—a world, that is, which is replete with other beings to encounter, and meanings to fulfill.

Such a view is profoundly opposed to those motivational theories which are based on the homeostasis principle. These theories depict man as if he were a closed system. According to them, man is basically concerned with maintaining or restoring an inner equilibrium, and to this end with the reduction of tensions. In the final analysis, this is also assumed to be the goal of the gratification of drives and the satisfaction of needs. As Charlotte Bühler[1] has rightly pointed out, "from Freud's

[1] Charlotte Bühler, "Basic Tendencies in Human Life: Theoretical and Clinical Considerations," in *Sein und Sinn*, edited by R. Wisser, Tübingen, 1960.

earliest formulations of the pleasure principle, to the latest present version of the discharge of tension and homeostasis principle, the unchanging end-goal of all activity all through life was conceived of as the re-establishment of the individual's equilibrium."

The pleasure principle serves the purpose of the homeostasis principle; but also, in turn, the purpose of the pleasure principle is served by the reality principle. According to Freud's statement, the goal of the reality principle is to secure pleasure, albeit delayed.

Von Bertalanffy could show that even within biology the homeostasis principle is no longer tenable. Goldstein could offer evidence, on the grounds of brain pathology, for his contention that the pursuit of homeostasis, rather than being a characteristic of the normal organism, is a sign of disorder. Only in cases of disease is the organism intent on avoiding tensions at any rate. In the field of psychology, Allport[2] objected to the homeostasis theory and said that it "falls short of representing the nature of propriate striving" whose "characteristic feature is its resistance to equilibrium: tension is maintained rather than reduced." Maslow[3] as well as Charlotte Bühler[4] have aired similar objections. In a more recent study, Charlotte Bühler[5] stated that "according to Freud's homeostasis principle, the ultimate goal was to obtain that kind of full gratification which would restore the individual's equilibrium in bringing all his desires to rest. From this point of view, all cultural creations of humanity become actually by-

[2] Gordon W. Allport, *Becoming: Basic Considerations for a Psychology of Personality,* Yale University Press, New Haven, 1955.

[3] Abraham H. Maslow, *Motivation and Personality,* Harper & Brothers, New York, 1954.

[4] Charlotte Bühler, "Theoretical Observations about Life's Basic Tendencies," *American Journal of Psychotherapy* 13: 561, 1959.

[5] Charlotte Bühler, "The Human Course of Life in its Goal Aspects," *Journal of Humanistic Psychology* 4: 1, 1964.

products of the drive for personal satisfaction." But even with a view to future reformulations of the psychoanalytic theory, Charlotte Bühler[6] is doubtful because, as she says, "the psycho-analytic theory can, in spite of all attempts to renew it, never get away from its basic hypothesis that the primary end-goal of all striving is homeostatic satisfaction. Creating values and accomplishing things are secondary goals, due to the overcoming of the id by the ego and superego, but, again, ultimately serving satisfaction." In contrast, Charlotte Bühler "conceives of man as living with intentionality, which means living with purpose. The purpose is to give meaning to life . . . The individual . . . wants to create values." Even more, "the human being" has "a primary, or native orientation, in the direction of creating and of values."

Thus the homeostasis principle does not yield a sufficient ground on which to explain human behavior. Particularly such human phenomena as the creativity of man, which is oriented toward values and meaning, are scotomized in such a frame of reference.

As for the pleasure principle, I would go even further in my criticism. It is my contention that, in the final analysis, the pleasure principle is self-defeating. The more one aims at pleasure, the more his aim is missed. In other words, the very "pursuit of happiness" is what thwarts it. This self-defeating quality of pleasure-seeking accounts for many sexual neuroses. Time and again the psychiatrist is in a position to witness how both orgasm and potency are impaired by being made the target of intention. This occurs all the more if, as is frequently the case, excessive intention is associated with excessive attention. Hyper-intention and hyper-reflection, as I am used to calling them, are likely to create neurotic patterns of behavior.

[6] Charlotte Bühler, "Some Observations on the Psychology of the Third Force," *Journal of Humanistic Psychology* 5: 54, 1965.

Normally pleasure is never the goal of human strivings but rather is, and must remain, an effect, more specifically, the side effect of attaining a goal. Attaining the goal constitutes a reason for being happy. In other words, if there is a reason for happiness, *happiness ensues*, automatically and spontaneously, as it were. And that is why *one need not pursue happiness*, one need not care for it once there is a reason for it.

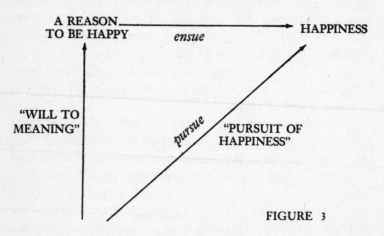

FIGURE 3

But, even more, *one cannot pursue it*. To the extent to which one makes happiness the objective of his motivation, he necessarily makes it the object of his attention. But precisely by so doing he loses sight of the reason for happiness, and happiness itself must fade away.

The accent which Freudian psychology places upon the pleasure principle is paralleled by the emphasis which Adlerian psychology places upon the status drive. However, this striving also proves to be self-defeating, insofar as a person who displays and exhibits his status drive will sooner or later be dismissed as a status seeker.

One personal experience of my own may help to illustrate this point. If any of my twenty-three books has become a success it has been that book which I initially planned to publish anonymously. Only after I had completed the manuscript was I persuaded by friends to let the publisher put my name on the book.[7] Is it not remarkable that precisely that book which I wrote under the conviction that it would not, that it could not, bring in success and fame, precisely this book actually became a success. May this serve as an illustration and admonition for young writers to obey their scientific or artistic conscience, as the case may be, and not to care for success. Success and *happiness* must *happen*, and the less one cares for them, the more they can.

In the final analysis, the status drive or the will to power, on one hand, and the pleasure principle or, as one might term it as well, the will to pleasure, on the other hand, are mere derivatives of man's primary concern, that is, his will to meaning—the second within the triad of concepts on which logotherapy is based. What I call the will to meaning could be defined as the basic striving of man to find and fulfill meaning and purpose.

But what is the justification of calling the will to power and the will to pleasure mere derivatives of the will to meaning? Simply that pleasure, rather than being an end of man's striving, is actually the effect of meaning fulfillment. And power, rather than being an end in itself, is actually the means to an end; if man is to live out his will to meaning, a certain amount of power—say, financial power—by and large will be an indispensable prerequisite. Only if one's original concern with meaning fulfillment is frustrated is one either *content with power* or *intent on pleasure*.

---

[7] Still the name of the author was not printed on the jacket when the original edition was published in German.

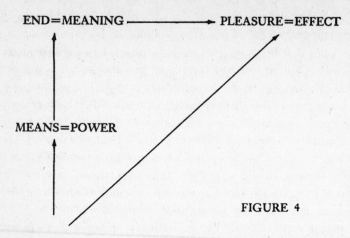

FIGURE 4

Both happiness and success are mere substitutes for fulfillment, and that is why the pleasure principle as well as the will to power are mere derivatives of the will to meaning. As their development is based on a neurotic distortion of man's original motivation, it is understandable that the founders of the classical psychotherapeutic schools who had to deal with neurotics developed their motivational theories solely on the grounds of those typically neurotic motivations which they observed when treating their patients.

So the hyperintention of pleasure might be traced to the frustration of another, more basic, concern. Let me illustrate this by a joke. A man meets his family doctor on the street. "How are you, Mr. Jones?" asks the doctor. "Pardon?" asks the man. "HOW ARE YOU?" asks the doctor again. "You see," answers the man, "my hearing capacity has deteriorated." Now it was the doctor's turn. "Certainly you are drinking too much. Stop drinking and you will hear better."

Some months later they meet again. "HOW ARE YOU, MR. JONES?" "You need not shout at me, Doctor. I am hearing quite well." "Certainly you have stopped drinking?" "That is true." Some months later they meet for the third time. But again the doctor has to raise his voice in order to make himself understood. "Certainly you have resumed drinking?" he asks his patient. And the latter replies, "Listen, Doctor. First I was drinking and my hearing became worse. Then I stopped drinking and heard better. But what I heard was not as good as whiskey."

This man had been frustrated by what he got to hear and that was why he returned to drinking. Since what he heard gave him no reason to be happy, he pursued happiness itself. Happiness even ensued because pleasure was brought about on a biochemical detour, by alcohol. As we know, pleasure cannot be attained by directly intending it. But as we now notice, it may well be obtained by a biochemical medium. Man, then, lacking a reason for pleasure, provides himself with a cause whose effect is pleasure. What is the difference between cause and reason? Reason is always something psychological or noological. Cause, however, is always something biological or physiological. If you cut onions you have no reason to weep; yet your tears have a cause. If you were in despair you would have a reason to weep. Or if a mountaineer attains a height of ten thousand feet and feels oppressed, his feeling may have either a reason or a cause. If he knows that he is badly equipped or poorly trained, his anxiety has a reason. But it may well be that it just has a cause—lack of oxygen.

Now let us return to the concept of a will to meaning. This is an assumption which is very compatible with Charlotte Bühler's[8] basic tendencies. For according to her theory, fulfillment is the final goal, and the four basic tendencies serve the

[8] Charlotte Bühler, "Theoretical Observations about Life's Basic Tendencies," *American Journal of Psychotherapy* 13: 561, 1959.

goal of fulfillment, provided that what is meant by fulfillment is the fulfillment of meaning rather than fulfillment of the self, or self-actualization.

Self-actualization is not man's ultimate destination. It is not even his primary intention. Self-actualization, if made an end in itself, contradicts the self-transcendent quality of human existence. Like happiness, self-actualization is an effect, the effect of meaning fulfillment. Only to the extent to which man fulfills a meaning out there in the world, does he fulfill himself. If he sets out to actualize himself rather than fulfill a meaning, self-actualization immediately loses its justification.

I would say self-actualization is the unintentional effect of life's intentionality. No one has ever put this more succinctly than the great philosopher Karl Jaspers when he said: "*Was der Mensch ist, das ist er durch die Sache, die er zur seinen macht*," or, as I would translate it into English, "What man is, he has become through that cause which he has made his own."

My contention that man loses any ground for self-actualization if he cares for it is perfectly in accordance with Maslow's own view, since he admits himself that the "business of self-actualization" can best be carried out "via a commitment to an important job."[9] In my view, excessive concern with self-actualization may be traced to a frustration of the will to meaning. As the boomerang comes back to the hunter who has thrown it only if it has missed its target, man, too, returns to himself and is intent upon self-actualization only if he has missed his mission.[10]

What is true of pleasure and happiness also holds for peak-experiences in the sense of Maslow's concept. They, too, are

[9] Abraham H. Maslow, *Eupsychian Management: A Journal*, R. Irwin, Homewood, Illinois, 1965, p. 136.
[10] Viktor E. Frankl, *Psychotherapy and Existentialism: Selected Papers on Logotherapy*, Washington Square Press, New York, 1967.

and must remain effects. They, too, ensue and cannot be pursued. Maslow himself would agree with this statement since it is his own contention that "hunting peaks is a little like hunting happiness."[11] Even more, he concedes that "the word, peak-experiences, is a generalization."[12] However, this is still an understatement, because his concept is more than a generalization. In a way it is even an oversimplification. And the same holds for another concept, the pleasure principle. After all, pleasure is the same irrespective of what causes it. Happiness is the same irrespective of the reason to experience it. Again, it is Maslow himself who admits that "our inner experiences of happiness are very similar no matter what stimulates them."[13] And as to the peak-experiences, he makes a parallel statement to the effect that they are uniform although "the stimuli are very different: we get them from rock and roll, drug addiction and alcohol," yet "the subjective experience tends to be similar."

It is obvious that dealing with the uniform forms of experiences rather than with their different contents presupposes that the self-transcendent quality of human existence has been shut out. However, "at every moment," as Allport puts it, "man's mind is directed by some intention."[14] Spiegelberg also refers to intention as the "property of an act which points to an object."[15] He leans on Brentano's contention that "every psychical phenomenon is characterized by the reference to a

[11] Abraham H. Maslow, "Lessons from the Peak-Experiences," *Journal of Humanistic Psychology* 2: 9, 1962.

[12] Abraham H. Maslow, "Fusion of Facts and Values," Lecture read before the Association for the Advancement of Psychoanalysis on March 28, 1963.

[13] Abraham H. Maslow, "Lessons from the Peak-Experiences," *Journal of Humanistic Psychology* 2: 9, 1962.

[14] Gordon W. Allport, *Personality and Social Encounter,* Beacon Press, Boston, 1960, p. 60.

[15] Herbert Spiegelberg, *The Phenomenological Movement,* Nijhoff, The Hague, 1960, p. 719.

content, the directedness toward an object."[16] But even Maslow is aware of this intentional quality of human experience, as is evidenced by his statement that "there is in the real world no such thing as blushing without something to blush about," in other words, blushing always means "blushing in a context."[17]

From this we may see how important it is in psychology to view the phenomena "in a context," more specifically, to view phenomena such as pleasure, happiness, and peak-experiences in the context with their respective objects, that is to say, with the *reason* a person has to be happy, and the *reason* he has to experience peaks and pleasures. Cutting off the objects to which such experiences refer must eventuate in an impoverishment of psychology. That is why human behavior cannot be fully understood along the lines of the hypothesis that man cares for pleasure and happiness irrespective of the reason to experience them. Such a motivational theory brackets the reasons which are different from each other, in favor of the effect which is always the same. Actually man does not care for pleasure and happiness as such but rather for that which causes these effects, be it the fulfillment of a personal meaning or the encounter with a human being. This even holds true of an encounter with the Divine Being. From this it follows how skeptical we must be with respect to that form of peak-experiences which is induced by LSD or other sorts of intoxication. If chemical causes are substituted for spiritual reasons, the effects are mere artifacts. The shortcut winds up as a blind alley.

To the class of those phenomena which cannot be pursued but rather must ensue also belongs health and conscience. If

[16] Franz Brentano, *Psychologie vom empirischen Standpunkt*, Meiner, Leipzig, 1924, p. 125.
[17] Abraham H. Maslow, *Motivation and Personality*, Harper & Brothers, New York, 1954, p. 60.

we strive for a good conscience we are no longer justified in having it. The very fact has made us into Pharisees. And if we make health our main concern we have fallen ill. We have become hypochondriacs.

Speaking of the self-defeating quality inherent in the pursuit of pleasure, happiness, self-actualization, peak-experiences, health, and conscience brings to my mind that story according to which Solomon was invited by God to utter a wish. After pondering for a while, Solomon said that he wished to become a wise judge for his people. Thereupon God said: "Well, Solomon, I will fulfill your wish, and make you the wisest man who ever existed. But precisely because you did not care for long life, health, wealth, and power, I will grant them to you in addition to what you wished for, and along with making you the wisest man, I will also make you the mightiest king who ever existed." Thus Solomon received the very gifts which he had not intended.

In principle, it would be justified to assume, as Ungersma[18] does, that the Freudian pleasure principle is the guiding principle of the small child, the Adlerian power principle is that of the adolescent, and the will to meaning is the guiding principle of the mature adult. "Thus," he says, "the development of the three schools of Viennese psychotherapy may be seen to mirror the ontogenetic development of the individual from childhood to maturity." However, the main reason for stipulating such a sequence would be the fact that in the earliest stages of development there is no indication of a will to meaning. But this fact is no longer embarrassing as soon as we recognize that life is a *Zeitgestalt*, a time gestalt, and as such becomes something whole only after the life course has been completed. A certain

[18] Aaron J. Ungersma, *The Search for Meaning: A New Approach to Psychotherapy and Pastoral Psychology*, Foreword by Viktor E. Frankl, The Westminster Press, Philadelphia, 1961.

phenomenon may, therefore, form a constitutive aspect of humanness and yet manifest itself only in an advanced stage of development.[19] Let us consider another definitely human capacity, that of creating and using symbols. There is no doubt that it is a characteristic of humanness, although there is no one who has ever seen a newborn baby with a command of language.

I have said that man does not care for pleasure and happiness as such but rather for that which causes these effects. This is most noticeable in the case of unhappiness. Let us imagine that an individual is mourning the death of a beloved person and is offered some tablets of a tranquilizing drug to bring him relief from his depression. Except for the case of neurotic escapism, we may be sure that he will refuse to tranquilize his grief away, for he will argue that this will not change anything, the beloved will not be revived this way. In other words, the reason for being depressed will remain. Unless he is a neurotic individual, he will be concerned with the reason for his depression rather than with the removal of this depression. He will be realistic enough to know that closing one's eyes

---

[19] "I would contend," Edward M. Bassis says, "that the 'will to meaning' is as much a motive for the young as for older generations. The problem appears to be that we can only infer its existence until the age when a child develops a sufficient command of the language to corroborate our inferences. Phenomenologically, though, the evidence for the 'will to meaning' in the young appears to me to be convincing. From birth he is involved in a world that is continually offering new wonders to be discovered, relationships to be explored and experienced, and activities to be invented. The reason that the infant so eagerly seeks new experiences, experiments with himself and his environment, is continually creative and innovative and develops his human potentials is due to the 'will to meaning'. I challenge anyone to observe a one-year-old for a period of time and then explain his purposive behavior and *joie de vivre* on the basis of need satisfaction and drive reduction without being guilty of sub-humanizing the humanness of the young." Unpublished paper.

before an event does not do away with the event itself. And the scientist, I think, should be at least as realistic as man normally is, and explore the behavior of man in the context of its intentional referent.

Empirical corroboration of the will to meaning concept is offered by Crumbaugh and Maholick,[20] who state that "the trend of observational and experimental data is favorable to the existence of Frankl's hypothetical drive in man." This, however, brings up the question whether it is legitimate to speak of the will to meaning in terms of a "drive in man." I think not. For, if we saw in the will to meaning just another drive, man would again be seen as a being basically concerned with his inner equilibrium. Obviously, he would then fulfill meaning in order to satisfy a drive to meaning, that is to say, in order to restore his inner equilibrium. He would then fulfill meaning not for its own sake but rather for his sake.

But even apart from subscribing to the homeostasis principle, conceiving of man's primary concern in terms of a drive would be but an inaccurate description of the actual state of affairs. An unbiased observation of what goes on in man when he is oriented toward meaning would reveal the fundamental difference between being driven to something on the one hand and striving for something on the other. It is one of the immediate data of life experience that man is pushed by drives but pulled by meaning, and this implies that it is always up to him to decide whether or not he wishes to fulfill the latter. Thus, meaning fulfillment always implies decision-making.

Thus, I speak of a will to meaning to preclude a misinterpretation of the concept in terms of a drive to meaning. By no

[20] James C. Crumbaugh and Leonard T. Maholick, "The Case for Frankl's 'Will to Meaning,'" *Journal of Existential Psychiatry* 4: 43, 1963.

means is a voluntaristic bias involved in the terminology. It is true that Rollo May[21] has argued that "the existential approach puts decision and will back into the center of the picture," and after "the existential psychotherapists" are "concerned with the problems of will and decision as central to the process of therapy," "the very stone which the builders rejected has become the head of the corner." But I should like to add that we have also to take heed lest we relapse into preaching will power, or teaching voluntarism. Will cannot be demanded, commanded, or ordered. One cannot will to will. And if the will to meaning is to be elicited, meaning itself has to be elucidated.

Charlotte Bühler[22] believes that "the healthy organism's functioning depends on an alternation of discharging and of upholding tensions." I think that such an ontogenetic alteration is paralleled by a phylogenetic one. There are periods of increasing and decreasing tension which may also be observed in the history of humanity. Freud's age was a period of tension, brought about by the repression of sex on a mass scale. Now we live in an age of relief, and, in particular, of the release of sex. It was, in particular, people living in Anglo-Saxon countries who, due to their puritanism, had suffered for too long a period of time from the mass repression of sex. As pointed out in the first chapter, the service done to them by Freud caused them to feel indebted to him for life, and this lifelong indebtedness may well account for much irrational resistance against new approaches in psychiatry which go beyond psychoanalysis.

Today people are spared tension. First of all, this lack of

[21] Rollo May, "Will, Decision and Responsibility," *Review of Existential Psychology and Psychiatry* 1: 249, 1961.

[22] Charlotte Bühler, "Basic Tendencies in Human Life: Theoretical and Clinical Considerations," in *Sein und Sinn,* edited by R. Wisser, Tübingen, 1960.

tension is due to that loss of meaning which I describe as the existential vacuum, or the frustration of the will to meaning.

In an editorial included in the campus paper of the University of Georgia, Becky Leet asks the question: "For today's younger generation, how relevant is Freud or Adler? We've got The Pill to free us from the repercussions of sexual fulfillment—today there is no medical need to be frustrated and inhibited. And we've got power—witness the sensitivity of American politicians to the 25-and-under crowd or look at China's Red Guards. On the other hand, Frankl says that people today live in an existential vacuum and this existential vacuum manifests itself mainly in a state of boredom. Boredom—sounds familiar? How many people do you know who complain of being bored—even though we've got everything at our fingertips, including Freud's sex and Adler's power? It makes you wonder why. Frankl may have the answer."

Of course, he does not have the answer. After all, it is not the function of logotherapy to give answers. Its actual function is rather that of a catalyst. This function has been described by a young American who wrote to me from Vietnam: "I've not yet found an answer to my questions from your philosophy, but you've started my own wheels of self-analysis turning once again."

To what extent does education reinforce the existential vacuum and contribute to the lack of tension? An education that is still based on the homeostasis theory is guided by the principle that as few demands as possible should be imposed upon young people. It is true that young people should not be subjected to excessive demands. However, we have also to consider the fact that, at least today, in the age of an affluent society, most people suffer too few demands rather than too many. The affluent society is an underdemanding society by which people are spared tension.

However, people who are spared tension are likely to create it, either in a healthy or in an unhealthy way. As to the healthy way, it seems to me to be the function of sports to allow people to live out their need for tension by deliberately imposing a demand upon themselves, that demand which they are spared by the underdemanding society. Even more, some sort of asceticism seems to me to be involved in sports. Thus it is not justified to deplore, as the German sociologist Arnold Gehlen[23] does, that there is no secular equivalent substituting for the medieval virtue of asceticism.

As to the unhealthy way in which tension is created, particularly in young people, let us just think of the type of people who are called beatniks and hooligans. They provoke policemen, as is the case in Vienna; or, as is the case on the American East Coast, they "play chicken." These people are risking their lives in the same fashion as those who are addicted to surfriding, and, to this end, skip school and cut classes, as is the case on the American West Coast. It goes without saying that I restrict my contention to people who are addicted. People who are addicted to LSD take it for the same purpose, to get a thrill or a kick. In England, Mods and Rockers fight one another. In Oslo, vandalism is successfully countered by former vandals. Every night a dozen volunteers, aged fourteen to eighteen, guard Frogner Park's swimming pool and ride on Oslo's streetcars to prevent seat-slashing. Over half of the boys are onetime hooligans. "They find it just as exciting," reads the pertinent report, "to be on the side of the law as against it." That is to say, they had been in search of excitement and tension, that tension which they are spared by society.

Education avoids confronting young people with ideals and values. They are shunned. There is a feature of American

[23] Arnold Gehlen, *Anthropologische Forschung*, Rowohlt, Hamburg, 1961.

culture that is striking in the eyes of the European. I refer to the obsession to avoid being authoritarian, to avoid even being directive. This obsession may be traced to puritanism, a moral and ethical authoritarianism and totalitarianism. The obsession not to confront young people with ideals and values might well be a reaction formation.

The collective obsessive fear that meaning and purpose might be imposed upon ourselves has resulted in an idiosyncrasy against ideals and values. Thus, the baby has been dumped out along with the bathwater, and ideals and values have been dismissed altogether. However, the head of the Department of Psychiatry, Neurology, and Behavioral Sciences at the University of Oklahoma School of Medicine, L. J. West,[24] only recently made the following statement: "Our youth can afford idealism because they are the first generation of the affluent society. Yet they cannot afford materialism—dialectical or capitalistic—because they are the first generation that might truly see the end of the world. Our young men and women are educated enough to know that only an ideal of human brotherhood can save their world and them." Apparently they are. Let me just quote the Austrian Trade Union which conducted a public opinion poll. It turned out that 87 percent of fifteen hundred young people who had been screened expressed their conviction that, indeed, it is worthwhile to have ideals. Even on a mass scale, "ideals are the very stuff of survival," to quote, for a change, instead of more depth psychologists, a height psychologist as it were, John H. Glenn.[25]

Contrary to the homeostasis theory, tension is not something to avoid unconditionally, and peace of mind, or peace of soul,

[24] Louis Jolyon West, "Psychiatry, 'Brainwashing,' and the American Character," *American Journal of Psychiatry* 120: 842, 1964.
[25] John H. Glenn, *The Detroit News*, February 20, 1963.

is not anything to avow unconditionally. A sound amount of tension, such as that tension which is aroused by a meaning to fulfill, is inherent in being human and is indispensable for mental well-being. What man needs first of all is that tension which is created by direction. Freud[26] once said that "men are strong as long as they stand for a strong idea." In fact, this has been put to the test both in Japanese and North Korean prisoner-of-war camps (Nardini[27] and Lifton,[28] respectively), as well as concentration camps. Even under normal conditions, a strong meaning orientation is a health-promoting and a life-prolonging, if not a life-preserving, agent. It not only makes for physical but also for mental health (Kotchen).[29]

Let me refer to what happened last year on the campus of the University of California at Berkeley. When the picketing started, the number of admissions to the psychiatric department of the student hospital suddenly dropped. And it sharply increased once the picketing was over. For some months students had found meaning in the freedom-of-speech movement.

Speaking of freedom brings to mind what happened to me years ago when I was lecturing at an American university. A famous American Freudian, commenting on a paper I had read, reported that he just had returned from Moscow. There, he said, he had found a lower frequency of neurosis as compared with the United States. He added that this might be traced to the fact that in Communist countries, as he felt, people are more often confronted with a task to complete. "This speaks in favor of your theory," he concluded, "that meaning direction

---

[26] Sigmund Freud, *Gesammelte Werke*, Vol.10, p. 113.

[27] J. E. Nardini, "Survival Factors in American Prisoners of War," *American Journal of Psychiatry* 109: 244, 1952.

[28] Robert J. Lifton, "Home by Ship: Reaction Patterns of American Prisoners of War Repatriated from North Korea," *American Journal of Psychiatry* 110: 732, 1954.

[29] Theodore A. Kotchen, "Existential Mental Health: An Empirical Approach," *Journal of Individual Psychology* 16: 174, 1960.

and task orientation are important in terms of mental health."

A year later, some Polish psychiatrists asked me to give a paper on logotherapy, and when I did so I quoted the American psychoanalyst. "You are less neurotic than the Americans because you have more tasks to complete," I told them. And they smugly smiled. "But do not forget," I added, "that the Americans have retained the freedom also to choose their tasks, a freedom which sometimes seems to me to be denied to you." They stopped smiling.

How fine it would be to synthesize East and West, to blend tasks with freedom. Freedom then could fully develop. It really is a negative concept which requires a positive complement.[30] And the positive complement is responsibleness. Responsibleness has two intentional referents. It refers to a meaning for whose fulfillment we are responsible, and also to a being before whom we are responsible. Therefore the sound spirit of democracy is but one-sidedly conceived of if understood as freedom without responsibleness.

Freedom threatens to degenerate into mere arbitrariness unless it is lived in terms of responsibleness. I like to say that the Statue of Liberty on the East Coast should be supplemented by a Statue of Responsibility on the West Coast.

[30] The same holds for many a concept underlying the protest movements. Much of the protesting really is anti-testing, fighting against something rather than offering a positive alternative to fight for.

WHAT IS MEANT BY MEANING?

✻ ✻ ✻ I have tried to convey that existence falters unless there is "a strong idea," as Freud put it, or a strong ideal to hold on to. To quote Albert Einstein, "the man who regards his life as meaningless is not merely unhappy but hardly fit for life."

However, existence is not only intentional but also transcendent. Self-transcendence is the essence of existence. Being human is directed to something other than itself. Under this "otherness," to quote Rudolf Allers,[1] also falls the "otherness" of the intentional referent to which human behavior is pointing. Thereby "the realm of the trans-subjective," again to quote Allers,[2] is constituted. However, it has become fashionable to dim this trans-subjectiveness. Under the impact of existentialism the emphasis has been placed upon the subjectiveness of being human. Really this is a misinterpretation of existentialism. Those authors who pretend to have overcome the dichotomy between object and subject are not aware that, as a truly phenomenological analysis would reveal, there is no

[1] Rudolf Allers, "The Meaning of Heidegger," *The New Scholasticism* 26: 445, 1962.
[2] Rudolf Allers, "Ontoanalysis: A New Trend in Psychiatry," *Proceedings of the American Catholic Philosophical Association*, 1961, p. 78.

such thing as cognition outside of the polar field of tension established between object and subject. These authors are used to speaking of "being in the world." Yet to understand this phrase properly, one must recognize that being human profoundly means being engaged and entangled in a situation, and confronted with a world whose objectivity and reality is in no way detracted from by the subjectivity of that "being" who is "in the world."

Preserving the "otherness," the objectiveness, of the object means preserving that tension which is established between object and subject. This tension is the same as the tension between the "I am" and the "I ought,"[3] between reality and ideal, between being and meaning. And if this tension is to be preserved, meaning has to be prevented from coinciding with being. I should say that it is the meaning of meaning to set the pace of being.

I like to compare this necessity with that story which is told in the Bible: When Israel wandered through the wilderness, God's glory preceded in the form of a cloud: only in this way was it possible that Israel was guided by God. Imagine, on the other hand, what would have happened if God's presence, symbolized by the cloud, had dwelt in the midst of Israel: instead of leading them, this cloud would have clouded everything, and Israel would have gone astray.

In this light one may see a risk in "the fusion of facts and values" as it takes place "in the peak-experiences and in self-actualizing people,"[4] since in the peak-experiences "the 'is' and the 'ought' merge with each other."[5] However, being human

[3] Viktor E. Frankl, *Psychotherapy and Existentialism: Selected Papers on Logotherapy*, Washington Square Press, New York, 1967.

[4] Abraham H. Maslow, *Eupsychian Management: A Journal*, R. Irwin, Homewood, Illinois, 1965.

[5] Abraham H. Maslow, "Lessons from the Peak-Experiences," *Journal of Humanistic Psychology* 2: 9, 1962.

means being in the face of meaning to fulfill and values to realize. It means living in the polar field of tension established between reality and ideals to materialize. Man lives by ideals and values. Human existence is not authentic unless it is lived in terms of self-transcendence.

Man's original and natural concern with meaning and values is endangered by the prevalent subjectivism and relativism. Both are liable to erode idealism and enthusiasm.

Let me draw your attention to the following example quoted from an American psychologist: "Charles . . . was especially 'angry' as he put it, when he would get a bill from a professional person such as a dentist or a physician, for service, and either made partial payments or none at all . . . My own personal attitude toward debts is quite different, and I place great value on paying my bills promptly. In this situation I did not discuss my own values, but focussed rather on the psychodynamics of his behavior because . . . my own compulsive need to pay promptly is neurotically motivated . . . Under no circumstances do I consciously attempt to direct or persuade the patient to adopt my values since I am convinced that values are . . . relative . . . rather than . . . absolute."[6]

I think paying one's bills may have a meaning irrespective of whether or not one likes it and irrespective of the unconscious meaning it may have. Gordon W. Allport once rightly said: "Freud was a specialist in precisely those motives that cannot be taken at their face value."[7] The fact that such motives exist certainly does not alter the fact that by and large motives can be taken at their face value. And if this is denied, what might be the unconscious and hidden motives behind the denial?

[6] James S. Simkin, in Charlotte Bühler, *Values in Psychotherapy*, Free Press of Glencoe, New York, 1962.

[7] Gordon W. Allport, *Personality and Social Encounter*, Beacon Press, Boston, 1960.

Let us take up a review published by Dr. Julius Heuscher on two volumes which a famous Freudian psychoanalyst devoted to Goethe. "In the 1,538 pages," the book review[8] reads, the author "portrays to us a genius with the earmarks of a manic-depressive, paranoid, and epileptoid disorder, of homosexuality, incest, voyeurism, exhibitionism, fetishism, impotence, narcissism, obsessive-compulsive neurosis, hysteria, megalomania, etc. . . . He seems to focus almost exclusively upon the instinctual dynamic forces that underlie . . . the artistic product. We are led to believe that [Goethe's work is] but the result of pregenital fixations. [His] struggle does not really aim for an ideal, for beauty, for values, but for the overcoming of an embarrassing problem of premature ejaculation . . . These volumes show us again," the author of the review concludes, "that the basic position [of psychoanalysis] has not really changed."

We now may understand how justified William Irwin Thompson was when he asked the question: "If the most educated members of our culture continue to look at geniuses as disguised sexual perverts, if they continue to think that all values are the specious fictions that are normative of collective man but not of the clever scientist who knows better, how can we be alarmed if the mass of our culture shows little regard for values and instead loses itself in an orgy of consumption, crime, and immorality?"[9]

Small wonder if this state of affairs takes its toll. Only recently Lawrence John Hatterer[10] pointed out that "many an

---

[8] Julius Heuscher, "Book Review," *Journal of Existentialism* 5: 229, 1964.
[9] William Irwin Thompson, "Anthropology and the Study of Values," *Main Currents in Modern Thought* 19: 37, 1962.
[10] Lawrence John Hatterer, "Work Identity: A New Psychotherapeutic Dimension," Annual Meeting, American Psychiatric Association. Quoted from *Psychiatric Spectator*, Vol. II, 7: 12, 1965.

artist has left a psychiatrist's office enraged by interpretations that he writes because he is an injustice collector or a sado-masochist, acts because he is an exhibitionist, dances because he wants to seduce the audience sexually, or paints to over-come strict bowel training by free smearing."

How wise and cautious was Freud when he once remarked that sometimes a cigar may be a cigar and nothing but a cigar. Or is this statement itself just a defense mechanism, just a way to rationalize his own cigar smoking? This would be a *regressus in infinitum*. After all we do not share "Freud's faith in the identity of 'determined' and 'motivated,'" to quote Mas-low,[11] who blamed Freud for having "made the mistake of identifying 'determined' with 'unconsciously motivated' as if there were no other determinants of behavior."

According to one definition, meanings and values are nothing but reaction formations and defense mechanisms. As for my-self, I would not be willing to live for the sake of my reaction formations, even less to die for the sake of my defense mecha-nisms.

But are meanings and values as relative and subjective as one believes them to be? In a sense they are, but in a different sense from that in which relativism and subjectivism conceives of them. Meaning is relative in that it is related to a specific person who is entangled in a specific situation. One could say that meaning differs first from man to man and second from day to day, indeed, from hour to hour.

To be sure, I would prefer to speak of the uniqueness, rather than relativeness, of meanings. Uniqueness, however, is a quality not only of a situation but even of life as a whole, since life is a string of unique situations. Thus man is unique in terms of both essence and existence. In the final analysis, no one can

[11] Abraham H. Maslow, *Motivation and Personality*, Harper & Brothers, New York, 1954, p. 294.

be replaced—by virtue of the uniqueness of each man's essence. And each man's life is unique in that no one can repeat it—by virtue of the uniqueness of his existence. Sooner or later his life will be over forever, together with all the unique opportunities to fulfill the meanings.

I have nowhere found this couched in more precise and concise words than those of Hillel, the great Jewish sage who lived nearly two millennia ago. He said, "If I don't do it—who will do it? And if I don't do it right now—when should I do it? But if I do it for my own sake only—what am I?" If I don't do it . . . This seems to me to refer to the uniqueness of my own self. If I don't do it right now . . . refers to the uniqueness of the passing moment which gives me an opportunity to fulfill a meaning. And if I do it for my own sake only . . . what here comes in is no more nor less than the self-transcendent quality of human existence. The question, What am I if I do it for my own sake only—requires the answer: In no event a truly human being. For it is a characteristic constituent of human existence that it transcends itself, that it reaches out for something other than itself. To put it in Augustinian terms, man's heart is restless unless he has found, and fulfilled, meaning and purpose in life. This statement, as we will see in the next chapter, epitomizes much of the theory and therapy of that type of neurosis which I have termed noogenic.

But let us return to the uniqueness of meanings. From what I have said, it follows that there is no such thing as a universal meaning of life but only the unique meanings of the individual situations. However, we must not forget that among these situations there are also situations which have something in common, and consequently there are also meanings which are shared by human beings across society and, even more, throughout history. Rather than being related to unique situations these meanings refer to the human condition. And these meanings are what is understood by values. So that one may define values as those meaning universals which crystallize in the typical situations a society or even humanity has to face.

The possession of values alleviates man's search for meaning, because at least in typical situations he is spared making decisions. But, alas, he has also to pay for this relief, for in contrast to the unique meanings pertaining to unique situations it may well be that two values collide with one another. And value collisions are mirrored in the human psyche in the form of value conflicts and as such play an important part in the formation of noogenic neuroses.

FIGURE 5

Let us imagine that unique meanings are points, while values are circles. It is understandable that two values may overlap with one another, whereas this cannot happen to unique meanings (see Fig. 5). But we must ask ourselves whether two values can really collide with one another, in other words, whether their analogy with two-dimensional circles is correct. Would it not be more correct to compare values with three-dimensional spheres? Two three-dimensional spheres projected out of the three-dimensional space down into the two-dimensional plane may well yield two two-dimensional circles overlapping one another, although the spheres themselves do not even touch on one another (see Fig. 6). The impression that two values collide with one another is a consequence of the fact that a whole dimension is disregarded. And what is this dimension? It is the hierarchical order of values. According to Max Scheler, valuing implicitly means preferring one value to another. This is the final result of his profound phenomenological analysis of valuing processes. The rank of a value is experienced together with the value itself. In other words, the experience of one value includes the experience that it ranks higher than another. There is no place for value conflicts.

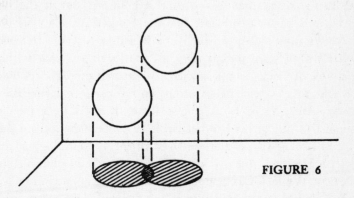

FIGURE 6

However, the experience of the hierarchical order of values does not dispense man from decision-making. Man is pushed by drives. But he is pulled by values. He is always free to accept or to reject a value he is offered by a situation. This is also true of the hierarchical order of values as it is channeled by moral and ethical traditions and standards. They still have to stand a test, the test of man's conscience—unless he refuses to obey his conscience and suppresses its voice.

Now that we have dealt with the question of how meanings are relative, let us proceed to the question of whether or not they are subjective. Is it not true that in the final analysis meanings are a matter of interpretation? And does not an interpretation always imply a decision? Are there not situations which allow for a variety of interpretations among which one has to

THE WILL TO MEANING

make a choice? An experience of my own suggests that there are.[12]

Shortly before the United States entered World War II I received an invitation from the American Embassy in Vienna to go there to pick up my visa for immigration to this country. At that time I was living in Vienna alone with my old parents. They, of course, did not expect me to do anything but pick up the visa and then hurry to this country. But at the last moment I began to hesitate because I asked myself, "Should I really? Can I do it at all?" For it suddenly came to mind what was in store for my parents, that is to say, that within a couple of weeks, as the situation was at that time, they would be sent to a concentration camp, or rather, an extermination camp. And should I really just leave them to their fate in Vienna? Until then I had been able to protect them from this fate because I was head of the Department of Neurology at the Jewish Hospital. But if I left the situation would immediately change. While I was pondering what my true responsibility was, I felt that this was that type of situation in which you wish for what is usually called a hint from Heaven. Then I went home and when I did so, I noticed a piece of marble stone lying on a table. I inquired of my father how it came to be there, and he said, "Oh, Viktor, I picked it up this morning at the site where the synagogue stood." (It had been burned down by the National Socialists.) "And why did you take it with you?" I asked him. "Because it is a part of the two tables containing the Ten Commandments." And he showed me, on the marble stone, a Hebrew letter engraved and gilded. "And I can tell you even more," he continued, "if you are interested; this Hebrew letter serves as the abbreviation of only one of

[12] Viktor E. Frankl, "Luncheon Address to the Third Annual Meeting of the Academy of Religion and Mental Health," *Journal of Existential Psychiatry* 4: 27, 1963.

the Ten Commandments." Eagerly I asked him, "Which one?" And his answer was: "Honor father and mother and you will dwell in the land." On the spot I decided to stay in the country, together with my parents, and let the visa lapse.

You are fully justified in claiming that this was a projective test, that I must have made my decision in the depth of my heart beforehand and just projected it into the appearance of a piece of marble stone. But if I had seen in the piece of marble stone nothing but calcium carbonate, this too would have been the result of a projective test, more specifically, the expression of a sense of meaninglessness, or of that inner emptiness and void which I have termed the existential vacuum.

Thus, to all appearances, meaning is just something we are projecting into the things around ourselves, things which in themselves are neutral. And in the light of this neutrality, reality may well seem to be just a screen upon which we are projecting our own wishful thinking, a Rorschach blot, as it were. If that were so, meaning would be no more than a mere means of self-expression, and thus something profoundly subjective.[13]

However, the only thing which is subjective is the perspective through which we approach reality, and this subjectiveness does not in the least detract from the objectiveness of reality itself. I improvised an explanation of this phenomenon for the students in my seminar at Harvard. "Just look through the windows of this lecture hall at Harvard Chapel. Each of you sees the chapel in a different way, from a different perspective, depending on the location of your seat. If anyone claimed that he sees the chapel exactly as his neighbor does, I would

[13] Cf. Kai Nielsen, "Linguistic Philosophy and Beliefs," *Journal of Existentialism* 6: 421, 1966, who says that "life does not have a meaning that is there to be discovered . . . but it has whatever meaning we give it." He leans upon a similar statement made by A. J. Ayer, "Deistic Fallacies," *Polemic* 1: 19, 1946.

have to say that one of them must be hallucinating. But does the difference of views in the least detract from the objectivity and reality of the chapel? Certainly it does not."

Human cognition is not of kaleidoscopic nature. If you look into a kaleidoscope, you see only what is inside of the kaleidoscope itself. On the other hand, if you look through a telescope you see something which is outside of the telescope itself. And if you look at the world, or a thing in the world, you also see more than, say, the perspective. What is *seen through* the perspective, however subjective the perspective may be, is the objective world. In fact, "seen through" is the literal translation of the Latin word, *perspectum*.

I have no objection to replacing the term "objective" with the more cautious term "trans-subjective" as it is used, for example, by Allers.[14] This does not make a difference. Nor does it make a difference whether we speak of things or meanings. Both are "trans-subjective." This trans-subjectiveness has really been presupposed all along whenever we spoke of self-transcendence. Human beings are transcending themselves toward meanings which are something other than themselves, which are more than mere expressions of their selves, more than mere projections of these selves. Meanings are discovered but not invented.

This is opposed to the contention of Jean-Paul Sartre that ideals and values are designed and invented by man. Or, as Jean-Paul Sartre has it, man invents himself. This reminds me of a fakir trick. The fakir claims to throw a rope into the air, into the empty space, without anything to fix it on, and yet, he pretends, a boy will climb up the rope. Does not Sartre, too, try to make us believe that man "projects," this literally means

[14] Rudolf Allers, "Ontoanalysis: A New Trend in Psychiatry," *Proceedings of the American Catholic Philosophical Association*, p. 78, 1961.

throws forward and upward, an ideal into nothingness, and yet man can climb up to the actualization of this ideal and the perfection of his self? But that polar field of tension which man so badly needs in terms of mental health and moral wholeness cannot be established unless the objectiveness of the objective pole is preserved, and the trans-subjectiveness of meaning is experienced by that human being who has to fulfill this meaning.

That this trans-subjectiveness is in actual fact experienced by man is apparent from the form in which he speaks of this experience. Unless his self-understanding is crippled by preconceived patterns of interpretation, not to say indoctrination, he refers to meaning as something to find rather than something to give. And a phenomenological analysis which attempts to describe such an experience in an unbiased and empirical way will show us that, indeed, meanings are found rather than given. If given at all, I would say, they are not given in an arbitrary way but rather in the way in which answers are given. That is to say that to each question there is one answer—the right one. There is only one meaning to each situation, and this is its true meaning.

On one of my lecture tours through the United States my audience was requested to print questions in block letters for me to answer and hand them over to a theologian who passed them on to me. The theologian suggested that I skip one, for, as he said, it was "sheer nonsense. Someone wishes to know," he said, "how you define six hundred in your theory of existence." When I read the question I saw a different meaning. "How do you define GOD in your theory of existence?" Printed in block letters, "GOD" and "600" were hard to differentiate. Well, was not this an unintentional projective test? After all, the theologian read "600," and the neurologist read "GOD."[15] But only one way to read the question was the right one. Only one way to read the question was the way in which it was meant by him who had asked it. Thus we have arrived at a definition of what meaning is. *Meaning is what is meant*, be it by a person who asks me a question, or by a situation which, too, implies a question and calls for an answer. I cannot say, "My answer right or wrong," as the Americans say, "My country right or wrong." I must try hard to find out the true meaning of the question which I am asked.

To be sure, man is free to answer the questions he is asked by life. But this freedom must not be confounded with arbitrariness. It must be interpreted in terms of responsibleness. Man is responsible for giving the *right* answer to a question, for finding the *true* meaning of a situation. And meaning is something to be found rather than to be given, discovered rather than invented. Crumbaugh and Maholick[16] point out that finding meaning in a situation has something to do with a Gestalt perception. This assumption is supported by the Gestaltist Wertheimer's statement: "The situation, seven plus seven equals . . . is a system with a lacuna, a gap. It is possible to fill the gap in various ways. The one completion—fourteen—corresponds to the situation, fits the gap, is what is structurally demanded in this system, in this place, with its function in the whole. It does justice to the situation. Other completions, such as fifteen, do not fit. They are not the right ones. We have here the concepts of the demands of the situa-

---

[15] Later on, I also used it intentionally by making the facsimile into a slide and showing it to my American students at the University of Vienna. Believe it or not, 9 students read "600," another 9 students read "GOD," and 4 students undecidedly vacillated between both modes of interpretation.

[16] James C. Crumbaugh and Leonard T. Maholick, "The Case for Frankl's 'Will to Meaning,'" *Journal of Existential Psychiatry* 4: 43, 1963.

tion; the 'requiredness.' 'Requirements' of such an order are objective qualities."[17]

I have said that meaning cannot be given arbitrarily but must be found responsibly. I could have said as well that it must be sought for conscientiously. And in fact man is guided in his search for meaning by conscience. Conscience could be defined as the intuitive capacity of man to find out the meaning of a situation. Since this meaning is something unique, it does not fall under a general law, and an intuitive capacity such as conscience is the only means to seize hold of meaning Gestalts.

Apart from being intuitive, conscience is creative. Time and again, an individual's conscience commands him to do something which contradicts what is preached by the society to which the individual belongs, say, by his tribe. Suppose this tribe consists of cannibals; an individual's creative conscience may well find out that, in a given situation, it is more meaningful to spare the life of an enemy than to kill him. This way his conscience may well start a revolution, in that what is at first a unique meaning may become a universal value—"Thou shalt not kill." The unique meaning of today is the universal value of tomorrow. This it the way religions are created and values evolve.

Conscience also has the power to discover unique meanings that contradict accepted values. The Commandment I have just quoted is followed by another, "Thou shalt not commit adultery." What comes to mind, in this context, is the story of a man who, together with his young wife, was imprisoned in Auschwitz. When they came there, he told me after his liberation, and were separated from one another, he suddenly felt a

[17] M. Wertheimer, "Some Problems in the Theory of Ethics," in *Documents of Gestalt Psychology,* edited by M. Henle, University of California Press, Berkeley, 1961.

strong urge to implore her to survive "at any expense—you understand? At any cost . . ." She understood what he meant: she was a beauty, and there might be, in the near future, a chance for her to save her life by agreeing to prostitution among the SS. And if such a situation should arise, her husband wanted to give her his absolution, as it were, in advance. In the last moment, conscience had compelled and commanded him to dispense her from the Commandment, "You shalt not commit adultery." In the unique situation—indeed a unique one—the unique meaning was to abandon the universal value of marital faithfulness, to disobey one of the Ten Commandments. To be sure, this was the only way to obey another of the Ten Commandments—"Thou shalt not kill." Not giving her his absolution would have made him co-responsible for her death.

Today we live in an age of crumbling and vanishing traditions. Thus, instead of new values being created by finding unique meanings, the reverse happens. Universal values are on the wane. That is why ever more people are caught in a feeling of aimlessness and emptiness or, as I am used to calling it, an existential vacuum. However, even if all universal values disappeared, life would remain meaningful, since the unique meanings remain untouched by the loss of traditions. To be sure, if man is to find meanings even in an era without values, he has to be equipped with the full capacity of conscience. It therefore stands to reason that in an age such as ours, that is to say, in an age of the existential vacuum, the foremost task of education, instead of being satisfied with transmitting traditions and knowledge, is to refine that capacity which allows man to find unique meanings. Today education cannot afford to proceed along the lines of tradition, but must elicit the ability to make independent and authentic decisions. In an age in which the Ten Commandments seem to lose their unconditional validity, man must learn more than ever to listen to the ten thousand commandments arising from the ten thousand unique situations of which his life consists. And as to *these* commandments, he is referred to, and must rely on, his conscience. A lively and vivid conscience is also the only thing that enables man to resist the effects of the existential vacuum, namely, conformism and totalitarianism (see page 83).

We live in an age of affluence in many respects. The mass media bombard us with stimuli and we have to protect ourselves against them by filtering them, as it were. We are offered a lot of possibilities and have to make our choice among them. In short, we have to make decisions as to what is essential and what is not.

We live in an age of the Pill. We are offered unprecedented possibilities and unless we wish to be submerged and drowned in promiscuity we have to resort to selectivity. Selectivity, however, is based on responsibility, that is to say, on decision-making under the guidance of conscience.

True conscience has nothing to do with what I would term "superegotistic pseudomorality." Nor can it be dismissed as a conditioning process. Conscience is a definitely human phenomenon. But we must add that it is also "just" a human phenomenon. It is subject to the human condition in that it is stamped by the finiteness of man. For he is not only guided by conscience in his search for meaning, he is sometimes misled by it as well. Unless he is a perfectionist, he also will accept this fallibility of conscience.

It is true, man is free and responsible. But his freedom is finite. Human freedom is not omnipotence. Nor is human wisdom omniscience, and this holds for both cognition and conscience. One never knows whether or not it is the true meaning to which he is committed. And he will not know it even on his deathbed. *Ignoramus et ignorabimus*—we do not, and shall never know—as Emil Du Bois-Reymond once put it, albeit in a wholly different context of the psychophysical problem.

But if man is not to contradict his own humanness, he has to obey his conscience unconditionally, even though he is aware of the possibility of error. I would say that the *possibility of error* does not dispense him from the *necessity of trial*. As Gordon W. Allport puts it, "we can be at one and the same time half-sure and whole-hearted."[18]

The possibility that my conscience errs implies the possibility that another one's conscience is right. This entails humility and modesty. If I am to search for meaning, I have to be certain that there is meaning. If, on the other hand, I cannot be certain that I will also find it, I must be tolerant. This does not imply by any means any sort of indifferentism. Being tolerant does not mean that I share another one's belief. But it does mean that I acknowledge another one's right to believe, and obey, his own conscience.

It follows that a psychotherapist must not impose a value on the patient. The patient must be referred to his own conscience. And if I am asked, as I am time and again, whether this neutralism would have to be maintained even in the case of Hitler, I answer in the affirmative, because I am convinced that Hitler would never have become what he did unless he had *suppressed* within himself the voice of conscience.

It goes without saying that in emergency cases the psychotherapist need not stick to his neutralism. In the face of a suicidal risk it is perfectly legitimate to intervene because only an erroneous conscience will ever command a person to commit suicide. This statement parallels my conviction that only an erroneous conscience will ever command a person to com-

[18] Gordon W. Allport, "Psychological Models for Guidance," *Harvard Educational Review* 32: 373, 1962.

mit homicide, or—once more to refer to Hitler—genocide. But also apart from this assumption, the very Hippocratic oath would compel the doctor to prevent the patient from committing suicide. I am personally glad to take the blame for having been directive along the lines of a life-affirming *Weltanschauung* whenever I have had to treat a suicidal patient.

As a rule, however, the psychotherapist will not impose a *Weltanschauung* on the patient. The logotherapist is no exception. No logotherapist has claimed that he has the answers. It was not a logotherapist but "the serpent" who "said to the woman, 'you . . . will be like God, who knows good and bad.' " No logotherapist has pretended that he knows what is value and what is not, what has meaning and what has not, what makes sense and what does not.

Redlich and Freedman[19] dismiss logotherapy as an attempt to give a meaning to the patient's life. Actually, the reverse is true. I for one do not tire of making it a point that meaning must be found but cannot be given, least of all by the doctor.[20, 21] The patient must find it spontaneously. Logotherapy does not dispense and distribute prescriptions. Despite the fact that I have repeatedly made this clear, logotherapy is accused, time and again, of "giving meaning and purpose." Nobody accuses Freudian psychoanalysis, which is concerned with the patient's sexual life, of providing him with girls. No one accuses Adlerian psychology, which is concerned with the patient's social life, of providing him with jobs. Why is it, then, that

[19] F. C. Redlich and Daniel X. Freedman, *The Theory and Practice of Psychiatry,* Basic Books, New York, 1966.

[20] Viktor E. Frankl, "The Concept of Man in Logotherapy," *Journal of Existentialism* 6: 53, 1965.

[21] Viktor E. Frankl, "Logotherapy and Existential Analysis—A Review," *American Journal of Psychotherapy* 20: 252, 1966.

logotherapy, which is concerned with the patient's existential aspirations and frustrations, is charged with "giving meanings"?

This denunciation of logotherapy is even less understandable in the face of the fact that even *finding* meanings is a concern restricted to the field of noogenic neuroses, which accounts for only about 20 percent of the case material accruing to our clinics and offices. And there are scarcely any meaning problems and value conflicts at all involved in the paradoxical intention technique—an aspect of logotherapy developed for the treatment of psychogenic neuroses.

It is not the logotherapeutic but rather the psychoanalytic practitioner who, again to quote from the *International Journal of Psycho-Analysis*, "is a moralist first and foremost," in that "he influences people in regard to their moral and ethical conduct."[22] I personally believe that the moralistic dichotomy between egotism and altruism is obsolete. I am convinced that the egotist can only benefit from considering others, and conversely, the altruist—for the very sake of the others—must always take care of himself. I am sure that the moralistic approach will finally give way to an ontological approach. Such an approach would define good and bad in terms of what promotes, or blocks, the fulfillment of meaning irrespective of whether it is one's own meaning or that of someone else.

It is true that we logotherapists are convinced, and if need be, persuade our patients, that *there is* a meaning to fulfill. But we do not pretend to know *what* the meaning is. The reader may notice that we arrive at the third tenet of logotherapy—along with the freedom of will and the will to meaning: the meaning of life. In other words, our contention is that there is a meaning of life—a meaning, that is, for which man has been

[22] F. Gordon Pleune, "All Dis-Ease Is Not Disease: A Consideration of Psycho-Analysis, Psychotherapy, and Psycho-Social Engineering," *International Journal of Psycho-Analysis* 46: 358, 1965. Quoted from *Digest of Neurology and Psychiatry* 34: 148, 1966.

in search all along—and also that man has the freedom to embark on the fulfillment of this meaning.

But on what ground are we justified in assuming that life is, and remains, meaningful in every case? The ground I have in mind is not moralistic but simply empirical—in the broadest sense of the word. We need only turn to the way the man in the street actually experiences meanings and values and translate this into scientific language. Such an undertaking, I would say, is precisely the job to be carried out by what is called phenomenology. Conversely, it is the task of logotherapy to retranslate what we thus have learned into plain words so that we may teach our patients how they, too, may find meaning in life. One should not assume that this enterprise is based on explicitly philosophical discussions with our patients. There are other channels through which to get across to them that life is unconditionally meaningful. I well remember when, after a public lecture I had been invited to give by a University in New Orleans, I was approached by a man who just wanted to shake my hand and thank me. He was a true "man in the street," for he was a street construction worker who had been in prison for eleven years and the only thing that had upheld him inwardly was *Man's Search for Meaning*, a book he had found in the prison's library. So logotherapy is not a merely intellectual matter.

The logotherapist is neither a moralist nor an intellectual. His work is based on empirical, i.e., phenomenological, analyses, and a phenomenological analysis of the simple man in the street's experience of the valuing process shows that one can find meaning in life by creating a work or doing a deed or by experiencing goodness, truth, and beauty, by experiencing nature and culture; or, last but not least, by encountering another unique being in the very uniqueness of this human being—in other words, by loving him. However, the noblest appreciation of meaning is reserved to those people who, deprived of the opportunity to find meaning in a deed, in a work, or in love, by the very attitude which they choose to this predicament, rise above it and grow beyond themselves. What matters is the stand they take—a stand which allows for transmuting their predicament into achievement, triumph, and heroism.

If one prefers in this context to speak of values, he may discern three chief groups of values. I have classified them in terms of creative, experiential and attitudinal values. This sequence reflects the three principal ways in which man can find meaning in life. The first is what *he gives* to the world in terms of his creations; the second is what *he takes* from the world in terms of encounters and experiences; and the third is *the stand he takes* to his predicament in case he must face a fate which he cannot change. This is why life never ceases to hold a meaning, for even a person who is deprived of both creative and experiential values is still challenged by a meaning to fulfill, that is, by the meaning inherent in the right, in an upright way of suffering.

By way of illustration I would like to quote Rabbi Earl A. Grollman who once "received a call from a woman dying of an incurable disease. 'How can I meet the thought and reality of death?' she asked." The rabbi reports: "We spoke on numerous occasions and, as a rabbi, I introduced many of the concepts of immortality found in our faith. As an afterthought, I also mentioned the attitudinal value concept of Dr. Frankl. Much of the theological discussion made little impression upon her, but attitudinal values invited her curiosity—especially when she learned that the founder of this concept was a psychiatrist who was incarcerated in a concentration camp. This man and his teaching captured her imagination for he knew more than just the theoretical application of suffering. She resolved then and there if she could not avoid the inescapable suffering, she would determine the manner and mode in which she would meet the illness. She became a tower of strength to those around her, whose hearts were lacerated with pain. At first it was a 'bravado,' but with the passage of time the act became invested with purpose. She confided to me: 'Perhaps my single act of immortality might be in the way I face this adversity. Even though my pain at times is unbearable—I have achieved an inner peace and contentment that I had never known before.' She died in dignity and is remembered in our community for her indomitable courage."

I do not wish in this context to elaborate on the relationship between logotherapy and theology.[23] This subject is reserved to the last chapter of the book. Suffice it to say that in principle the attitudinal value concept is tenable whether or not a religious philosophy of life is espoused. The attitudinal value concept does not result from a moral or ethical prescription, but rather from an empirical and factual description of what goes on in man whenever he values his own or another's behavior. Logotherapy is based on *statements about values as facts* rather than on *judgments about facts as values*. And it is a fact that the man on the street values one who shoulders his cross with "indomitable courage" (to quote Rabbi Grollman) more than one who is merely successful, even if he is extremely successful, be it in terms of a businessman's making money or in terms of a playboy's making love.

Here let me stress that I refer to only "a fate which cannot be changed." Accepting the suffering of a curable disease, of an operable cancer, would not yield any meaning. It would

23 Orlo Strunk, "Religious Maturity and Viktor E. Frankl," in *Mature Religion*, Abingdon Press, New York, 1965; Earl A. Grollman, "Viktor E. Frankl: A Bridge Between Psychiatry and Religion," *Conservative Judaism* 19: 19, 1964; D. Swan Haworth, "Viktor Frankl," *Judaism* 14: 351, 1965.

constitute a form of masochism rather than heroism. But let me illuminate the point by a less abstract example. Once I came across an advertisement which was couched in the following poem whose translation into English I owe to my friend Joseph B. Fabry:

> Calmly bear, without ado,
> That which fate imposed on you;
> But to bedbugs don't resign:
> Turn for help to Rosenstein!

Richard Trautmann, in his book review[24] of my German book, *Homo patiens*,[25] was quite right in speaking of "suffering as something that has to be eliminated by all means and at all costs." However, one should assume that he, as an M.D., has become aware that sometimes there is unavoidable suffering confronting man, that man is a being which sooner or later must die and before doing so, must suffer—despite the advances of science so much worshipped by progressivism and scientism. Closing one's eyes before these existential "facts of life" means reinforcing our neurotic patients' escapism. Avoiding suffering as much as possible is desirable. But what about inescapable suffering? Logotherapy teaches that pain must be avoided as long as it is possible to avoid it. But as soon as a painful fate cannot be changed, it not only must be accepted but may be transmuted into something meaningful, into an achievement. I wonder if this approach actually "indicates a regressive tendency to self-destructive submissiveness," as Richard Trautmann contends.

[24] Richard Trautmann, "Book Review," *American Journal of Psychotherapy* 5: 821, 1952.
[25] Viktor E. Frankl, *Homo patiens: Versuch einer Pathodizee*, Franz Deuticke, Wien, 1950.

In a sense the attitudinal value concept is broader than that of meaning to be found in suffering. Suffering is only one aspect of what I call "the tragic triad" of human existence. This triad is made up of pain, guilt, and death. There is no human being who may say that he has not failed, that he does not suffer, and that he will not die.

The reader may notice that here the third "triad" is introduced. The first triad is constituted by freedom of will, will to meaning, and meaning of life. Meaning of life is composed of the second triad—creative, experiential, and attitudinal values. And attitudinal values are subdivided into the third triad—meaningful attitudes to pain, guilt, and death.

Speaking of the "tragic" triad should not mislead the reader to assume that logotherapy is as pessimistic as existentialism is said to be. Rather logotherapy is an optimistic approach to life, for it teaches that there are no tragic and negative aspects which could not be by the stand one takes to them transmuted into positive accomplishments.

But there is a difference between the attitudes one chooses to pain and guilt, respectively. In the case of pain, one really takes a stand to one's fate. Otherwise suffering would not yield meaning. In the case of guilt, however, the stand one takes is a stand to one's self. What is even more important, fate cannot be changed; otherwise it would not be fate. Man, however, may well change himself, otherwise he would not be man. It is a prerogative of being human, and a constituent of human existence, to be capable of shaping and reshaping oneself. In other words, it is a privilege of man to become guilty, and his responsibility to overcome guilt. As the editor of the *San Quentin News* put it in a letter to me, a man "could possibly undergo a transmutation" (see page 77).

No one has offered a more profound phenomenological analysis of such a transmutation than Max Scheler did in one

of his books,[26] more specifically, in the chapter on "Repent-
ance and Rebirth." As Max Scheler also pointed out, man has
a *right* to be considered guilty and to be punished. Once we
deal with man as the victim of circumstances and their influences, we not only cease to treat him as a human being but also
lame his will to change.

Let us turn to the third aspect of the tragic triad of human
existence, i.e., life's transitoriness. Usually man only sees the
stubble field of transitoriness and overlooks the full granaries
of the past. In the past, nothing is irrecoverably lost but everything irrevocably preserved and saved, safely delivered and
deposited. Nothing and nobody can deprive us of what we
have rescued into the past. What we have done cannot be
undone. This adds to man's responsibleness. For in the face of
the transitoriness of his life, he is responsible for using the
passing opportunities to actualize potentialities, to realize
values, whether creative, experiential, or attitudinal. In other
words, man is responsible for what to do, whom to love, and
how to suffer. Once he has realized a value, once he has fulfilled a meaning, he has fulfilled it once and forever.

But now let us return to both the simple man in the street
and the businessman, the first valuing the latter's success
"dimensionally" lower as compared with him who succeeds in
transmuting his predicament into an achievement. "Dimensional" anthropology, as outlined in a previous chapter, may
help us to understand what is meant by higher and lower.
Usually, in his everyday life, man lives, he moves, in a dimension whose positive pole is success and whose negative pole is
failure. This is the dimension of the competent man, of the
clever animal, of the *Homo sapiens*. But the *Homo patiens*,
the suffering man who by virtue of his humanness, is capable

[26] Max Scheler, *On the Eternal in Man,* Harper & Brothers, New
York, 1960.

of rising above, and taking a stand to, his suffering, moves in a dimension perpendicular to the former, as it were, a dimension whose positive pole is fulfillment and whose negative pole is despair. A human being strives for success but, if need be, does not depend on his fate, which does or does not *allow* for success. A human being, by the very attitude he chooses, is capable of finding and fulfilling meaning in even a hopeless situation. This fact is understandable only through our dimensional approach, which allots to the attitudinal values a higher dimension than to the creative and experiential values. The attitudinal values are the highest possible values. The meaning of suffering—unavoidable and inescapable suffering alone, of course—is the deepest possible meaning.

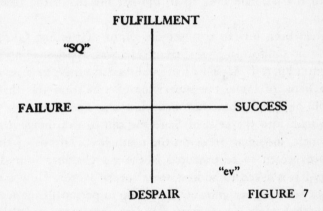

FIGURE 7

Rolf H. Von Eckartsberg conducted a study at Harvard University to investigate the life adjustment of Harvard's graduates. The result offers statistical evidence that among 100 subjects, who had graduated twenty years before, there was a huge percentage of people who complained of a crisis. They felt that their lives were pointless and meaningless—and this they did although they had been very successful in their professional lives—as lawyers, doctors, surgeons, and, last but not least, analysts, we may suppose—as well as in their marital lives. They were caught in an existential vacuum. In our diagram, they would have to be located at the point "e(existential) v(acuum)," below "success" and at the right side of "despair." A phenomenon such as the occurrence of *despair despite success* is explicable only along the lines of two different dimensions.

On the other hand, there is a phenomenon which could be described in terms of *fulfillment despite failure*. It is localized in the upper left angle. It is marked by "SQ," for San Quentin, because in this prison I once met a man who bears witness to my contention that meaning can be found in life literally up to the last moment, up to the last breath, in the face of death.

I had been invited to meet the editor of the *San Quentin News* at California State Prison. He was a prisoner at San Quentin himself. After he had published in his *News* a review of a book of mine, the supervisor of education felt that it would be wise to have him interview me. This interview was broadcast into the cells of San Quentin, to the thousands of prisoners, including those on the death row. To one of them who expected to be executed in the gas chamber four days later, I was asked to address some special words. How could I cope with this assignment? Resorting to personal experiences at another place where people had to face a gas chamber, I expressed my conviction that either life is meaningful—in which case its meaning does not depend upon its duration—or else it is meaningless, in which case it would be pointless to prolong it. I then spoke of Tolstoy's story "The Death of Ivan Ilyich." In this way I hoped to show the prisoners that man can rise above himself, grow beyond himself—even in the last moment—and by so doing retroactively invest meaning even in a wasted life. Believe it or not, the message reached the prisoners. Some time later I learned in a letter from an official at California State Prison that "the *San Quentin News* article that covered Doctor Frankl's visit to San Quentin took first place in a National Penal Press Journalism Contest sponsored by Southern Illinois University. The article was selected for top honors from a representative group composed of entries from more than 150 American correctional institutions." But after I had congratulated the prize winner by letter, he wrote to me that "the transcription of our discussion had been widely circulated within the institution" and that "there was some local criticism that went something like, 'It's fine in theory but life doesn't work that way.'" And then he confided to me the following: "I plan to write an editorial drawing from our current situation, our immediate predicament, showing that life does indeed work this way and I shall show them an exact circumstance from our prison where, from the depths of despair and futility a man was able to mold for himself a meaningful and significant life-experience. They, also, would not believe that a man under these circumstances could possibly undergo a transmutation which would turn despair into a triumph. I shall attempt to show them that not only is it a possibility, it is a necessity."

Let us take the lessons from both San Quentin and Harvard. People sentenced for life or waiting for death in gas chambers may "triumph," whereas the successful people followed up by Professor Von Eckartsberg fell in "despair." In the light of dimensional anthropology and ontology, despair is well compatible with success—as compatible as fulfillment of meaning is compatible with dying and suffering.

To be sure, once we project this fulfillment out of its own dimension into a dimension lower than its own, say, the dimension of the businessman or the playboy for whom *success* is what counts, once we project fulfillment of *meaning despite*, nay, because of, *suffering* into a lower dimension, it must become ambiguous—according to the second law of dimensional anthropology and ontology—and can be confounded with, say, "a regressive tendency to self-destructive submissiveness," to quote Richard Trautmann.[27]

Two American writers have studied the psychology of concentration camp prisoners. How do they interpret what these prisoners had to suffer? How is this suffering's meaning depicted after being projected into the dimension of analytic and dynamic psychologism? "The prisoners," one of the authors contends, "regressed to the narcissistic position. The tortures imposed"—what meaning do you expect that the prisoners' suffering from the tortures had? Listen: "The tortures imposed had the unconscious meaning of castration. The prisoners defended themselves via masochism, or sadism, and infantile behavior." Moreover: "Survivors of Nazi persecution repressed their rage against"—against whom do you expect them to have repressed their rage? "Against their murdered parents." And "the survivors attempt to ward off aggression against"—against whom? "Against their living children."

Even if we take it for granted that the case material is representative, it is obvious that the meaning of suffering eludes an attempt to understand it along the lines of purely analytic and dynamic interpretations.[28] Jürg Zutt, head of the Department of Psychiatry at the University of Frankfurt am Main, has pointed out that research in the field of the psychology of sur-

[27] Richard Trautmann, "Book Review," *American Journal of Psychotherapy* 5: 821, 1952.

[28] "To attempt to explain in psychodynamic terms the personality changes that follow exposure to extreme stress," F. Hocking says, "is to do a disservice to the unique contribution of Freud to the understanding of human behavior." F. Hocking, "Extreme Environmental Stress and Its Significance for Psychopathology," *American Journal of Psychotherapy* 24: 4, 1970.

vivors of Nazi persecution is not reliable because it is confined to a selected group of subjects.[29] Moreover, within the material furnished by any given case, only those aspects which fit in the analytic and dynamic model are selected. To refer to the "case" of a book of mine, *Man's Search for Meaning*, the only thing which attracted the attention of one reviewer of analytic and dynamic orientation was the fact that, as he felt, the prisoners regressed to the urethral stage of their libidinal development. Nothing but this he found worth being mentioned.

In conclusion, let us give a hearing to a man who should know better than psychoanalytical theorists—a man who as a boy was imprisoned in Auschwitz and left it when he still was a boy: Yehuda Bacon, one of Israel's leading artists, once published the following account of his experiences during the first period after his liberation from the concentration camp: "I remember one of my first impressions after the war—I saw a funeral with a huge coffin and music, and I started to laugh: 'Are they crazy, to make such a fuss over one corpse?' If I went to a concert or theater I would calculate how long it would take to gas a crowd of that size, how many clothes, how many gold teeth would be left, how many sacks of hair they would make." So far, Yehuda Bacon's suffering. Now—what was its meaning? "As a boy I thought: 'I will tell them what I saw, in the hope that people will change for the better.' But people didn't change and didn't even want to know. It was much later that I really understood the meaning of suffering. It can have a meaning if it changes *you* for the better."

[29] Jürg Zutt, "Book Review," *Jahrbuch für Psychologie, Psychotherapie und medizinische Anthropologie* 13; 362, 1965.

PART TWO

❧ ❧ ❧

APPLICATIONS OF
LOGOTHERAPY

THE EXISTENTIAL VACUUM:

A CHALLENGE TO

PSYCHIATRY

≱ ≱ ≱ AFTER dealing with meaning we now turn to
those people who suffer from a sense of meaninglessness and
emptiness. Ever more patients complain of what they call an
"inner void," and that is the reason why I have termed this
condition the "existential vacuum." In contradistinction to the
peak-experience so aptly described by Maslow, one could conceive of the existential vacuum in terms of an "abyss-experi-
ence."

The etiology of the existential vacuum seems to me to be a
consequence of the following facts. First, in contrast to an animal, no drives and instincts tell man what he *must* do. Second,
in contrast to former times, no conventions, traditions, and
values tell him what he *should* do; and often he does not even
know what he basically wishes to do. Instead he wishes to do
what other people do, or he does what other people wish him
to do. That is to say, he falls prey to conformism or totalitarianism, respectively, the first being representative for the West,
the second being representative for the East.

The existential vacuum is a phenomenon that is both increasing and spreading. Nowadays even Freudian psychoanalysts
admit, as was the case at an international meeting recently held
in West Germany, that more and more patients suffer from a

lack of content and purpose in life. Even more, they admit that this state of affairs accounts for many of the "unterminable analyses" because the treatment on the couch virtually becomes the only life content. Of course Freudian psychologists do not use the logotherapeutic term, the "existential vacuum," which I coined more than a decade ago; nor do they use logotherapeutic techniques to cope with the phenomenon. However, they do admit its existence.

The existential vacuum is not only increasing but also spreading. For example, a Czechoslovakian psychiatrist has pointed out, in a paper on existential frustration,[1] that the existential vacuum makes itself felt in Communist countries, too.

How, then, should we cope with the existential vacuum? One would assume that we have to espouse a sound philosophy of life in order to show that life really does hold a meaning, for each and every man. This assertion is based on the attitudinal value concept on which we elaborated in the last chapter, where we also pointed out that the wane of traditions affects only the universal values but not unique meanings.

But philosophy has been disdained by Sigmund Freud and dismissed by him as nothing but one of the most decent forms of the sublimation of repressed sexuality.[2] I personally believe that philosophy is not a mere sublimation of sex but rather that sex often serves as a cheap escape from precisely those philosophical and existential problems which beset man.

In an American magazine you may read the following statement: "Never, it is safe saying, in the history of the world has a country been so sex-ridden as America is today." Strangely

[1] S. Kratochvil, "K psychoterapii existencialni frustrace," *Československa psychiatria* 57: 186, 1961, and "K problemu existencialni frustrace," *Československa psychiatria* 62: 322, 1966.

[2] Ludwig Binswanger, *Erinnerungen an Sigmund Freud*, Francke, Bern, 1956.

enough, this statement is a quotation from *Esquire*. Anyway, if it is true, it would favor the hypothesis that the average American is also more caught in existential frustration than other people, and hence intent on sexual overcompensation. In this light one might understand that an improvised statistical survey conducted among my students at the University of Vienna Medical School showed that 40 percent of Austrian, West German, and Swiss students knew the existential vacuum from their own experience. Among those American students, however, who attended lectures I gave in English, it was not 40 but rather 81 percent.

The main manifestations of existential frustration—boredom and apathy—have become a challenge to education as well as to psychiatry. In an age of the existential vacuum, we have said, education must not confine itself to, and content itself with, transmitting traditions and knowledge, but rather it must refine man's capacity to find those unique meanings which are not affected by the crumbling of universal values. This human capacity to find meaning hidden in unique situations is conscience. Thus education must equip man with the means to find meanings. Instead, education often adds to the existential vacuum. The students' sense of emptiness and meaninglessness is reinforced by the way in which scientific findings are presented to them, by the reductionist way, that is. The students are exposed to an indoctrination along the lines of a mechanistic theory of man plus a relativistic philosophy of life.

A reductionist approach to man tends to reify him, that is to say, to deal with a human being as if he were a mere *res*, a thing. However, to quote William Irwin Thompson,[3] "humans are not objects that exist as chairs or tables; they live, and if they find that their lives are reduced to the mere existence of

[3] William Irwin Thompson, "Anthropology and the Study of Values," *Main Currents in Modern Thought* 19: 37, 1962.

chairs and tables, they commit suicide." This is by no means an overstatement. When I was lecturing at one of the major universities of this country, the dean of students, commenting on my paper, said that he could offer me a whole list of students who had clearly committed, or at least attempted to commit, suicide on the grounds of an existential vacuum. The existential vacuum had been a phenomenon familiar to him, confronting him day after day in his counseling practice.

I well remember how I felt when I was exposed to reductionism in education as a junior high school student at the age of thirteen. Once our natural science teacher told us that life in the final analysis was nothing but a combustion process, an oxidation process, I sprang to my feet and said, "Professor Fritz, if this is the case, what meaning then does life have?" To be sure, in his case one has not really to deal with an example of reductionism but ironically with an instance of what he would have to call oxidationism.

In this country many a leading figure in education has become concerned with the boredom and apathy apparent among students. For example, Edward D. Eddy, together with two associates, studied twenty representative colleges and universities in the United States, interviewing hundreds of administrators, faculty, and students. In his book, he arrived at the conclusion that "on almost every campus from California to New England, student apathy was a topic of conversation. It was the one subject mentioned most often in our discussions with both faculty members and students."[4]

In an interview with Professor Huston C. Smith, entitled "Value Dimensions in Teaching,"[5] Professor Smith, the philos-

---

[4] Edward D. Eddy, *The College Influence on Student Character,* American Council on Education, Washington, D.C., 1959.
[5] See page 16.

opher of Harvard, asked me whether it is possible to teach values. I answered that values cannot be taught; values must be lived. Nor can meaning be given; what a teacher can give to his students is not meaning but rather an example, the personal example of his own dedication and devotion to the cause of research, truth, and science. Then Professor Smith wanted me to discuss apathy and boredom, but I returned his question by asking him how can we expect the average American student to develop anything other than boredom and apathy? What else is boredom if not the incapacity to take an interest? And what else is apathy if not the incapacity to take the initiative? But how should a student take the initiative if he is taught that man is nothing but the battleground of the clashing claims of personality aspects such as id, ego, and superego? And how should a student take an interest, how could he care for ideals and values if one preaches that they are nothing but reaction formations and defense mechanisms? Reductionism can only undermine and erode the natural enthusiasm of youth. The enthusiasm and idealism of American youngsters must be simply inexhaustible; otherwise I cannot understand why so many of them are joining the Peace Corps and VISTA.

But how are we to deal with a given case of existential vacuum; not in prophylactic terms but rather in therapeutic terms? Does "dealing with" the existential vacuum imply that it is anything to treat? Is it a disease? Can we subscribe to a statement Sigmund Freud once made in a letter to Princess Bonaparte: "The moment one inquires about the sense or value of life, one is sick."[6]

Actually the misinterpretation of the existential vacuum as a pathological phenomenon is the result of its projection out of the noological space into the psychological plane. Accord-

[6] Sigmund Freud, *Briefe 1873–1939*, S. Fischer-Verlag, Frankfurt am Main, 1960.

ing to the Second Law of Dimensional Anthropology and Ontology, this procedure must entail and engender a diagnostic ambiguity. The difference between existential despair and emotional disease disappears. One cannot distinguish between spiritual distress and mental disease.

The existential vacuum is no neurosis; or, if it is a neurosis at all, it is a sociogenic neurosis, or even an iatrogenic neurosis—that is to say, a neurosis which is caused by the doctor who pretends to cure it. How often does a doctor explain away the patient's concern about an ultimate meaning of life in the face of death, by conceiving of "ultimate concern" as castration fear. To the patient it means a relief to know that he need not worry about the question of whether or not life is worth living, but may instead just face the fact that his Oedipal complex is not yet settled. To be sure, such an interpretation would constitute a rationalization of existential despair. (See page 125).

In this context I like to cite the case of a Viennese university professor who was admitted to my department because he doubted the meaning of life. As it soon turned out, he was actually suffering from an endogenous depression which according to traditional European psychiatry is somatogenic. But the most remarkable thing was that the patient was not haunted by his doubts during the depressive phases, but only during that time in which he was healthy. During the depressive phases he was too much occupied with hypochondriac complaints to concern himself with the meaning of life. Here we are confronted with a case in which existential despair and emotional disease proved to be mutually exclusive. Thus, it is hardly justified to dismiss the existential vacuum as "just another symptom" of neurosis.

However, although it need not be an effect of neurosis, the existential vacuum may well become its cause. We then speak of a noogenic neurosis in contradistinction to psychogenic and somatogenic neuroses. And we define the noogenic neurosis as a neurosis which is caused by a spiritual problem, a moral or ethical conflict, as for example, a conflict between the mere superego and the true conscience—the latter, if need be, contradicting and opposing the former. Last but not least, however, the noogenic etiology is formed by the existential vacuum, by existential frustration or by the frustration of the will to meaning.

James C. Crumbaugh, to his credit, developed a test, the Purpose-in-Life (PIL) test, to differentiate the noogenic neurosis from the conventional neuroses. Together with Leonard T. Maholick[7] he published the results he obtained and then delivered an amplified version before the annual meeting of the American Psychological Association. His data were based on a total of 1,151 subjects. Crumbaugh arrived at the conclusion that "noogenic neurosis exists apart from the conventional diagnostic categories [and is not] identical with any of the conventional diagnostic syndromes. [It represents] a new clinical syndrome which cannot be adequately comprehended under any of the classical descriptions. Present results lend support and are favorable to Frankl's concepts of noogenic neurosis and existential vacuum. The low correlation between the PIL and educational level implies on the one hand that purposeful, meaningful lives are not limited to those with educational opportunity, and on the other that education alone by no means assures the attainment of meaning in life."[8]

[7] James C. Crumbaugh and Leonard T. Maholick, "An Experimental Study in Existentialism: The Psychometric Approach to Frankl's Concept of Noogenic Neurosis," *Journal of Clinical Psychology* 20: 200, 1964.
[8] James C. Crumbaugh, "The Purpose-in-Life Test as a Measure of Frankl's Noogenic Neurosis," delivered before Division 24, American Psychological Association, New York City, September 3, 1966. A more detailed version of this paper was published in 1968 (James C. Crumbaugh,

Along with this empirical corroboration, statistical research has been conducted referring to the frequency of noogenic neurosis. Werner[9] in London, Langen and Volhard[10] in Tübingen, Prill[11] in Würzburg, and Niebauer[12] in Vienna agree that about 20 percent of the neuroses one encounters are noogenic in nature and origin.

Once the existential vacuum has eventuated in a noogenic neurosis it goes without saying that its treatment is reserved to the medical profession. In my home country, and in many countries, psychotherapy must not be practiced by anyone who is not a doctor of medicine. Of course, this legislation also holds for logotherapy. On the other hand it is understandable that those aspects of logotherapy which are not connected with the treatment of a disease, be it a noogenic, psychogenic, or somatogenic neurosis, are accessible to the other counseling professions as well. There is no reason why the clinical psychologist, the social worker, the pastor, priest, and rabbi should not offer advice and assistance to people who are seeking a meaning of life, or questioning the meaning of life: in other words, people in the grip of the existential vacuum. With this in mind, the Argentine Association of Existential Logotherapy,

---

"Cross-Validation of Purpose-in-Life Test Based on Frankl's Concepts," *Journal of Individual Psychology* 24: 74, 1968). A copy of the PIL used in this study will be sent upon request. Address the Psychology Service, Veterans Administration Hospital, Gulfport, Mississippi 39501.

[9] T. A. Werner, Opening paper read before the Symposium on Logotherapy, International Congress of Psychotherapy, Vienna, 1961.

[10] R. Volhard and D. Langen, "Mehrdimensionale Psychotherapie," *Zeitschrift für Psychotherapie* 3: 1, 1953.

[11] H. J. Prill, "Organneurose und Konstitution bei chronish-funktionellen Unterleibsbeschwerden der Frau," *Zeitschrift für Psychotherapie* 5: 215, 1955.

[12] K. Kocourek, E. Niebauer, and P. Polak, "Ergebnisse der klinischen Anwendung der Logotherapie," in *Handbuch der Neurosenlehre und Psychotherapie*, Vol. 3, edited by V. E. Frankl, V. E. von Gebsattel, and J. H. Schultz, Urban & Schwarzenberg, Munich-Berlin, 1959.

founded in 1954, built up a section for psychiatrists and another one for those of its members who are not M.D.'s.

Struggling for a meaning of life, or wrestling with the question of whether there is a meaning to life, is not in itself a pathological phenomenon. As to young people, it is their prerogative not to take it for granted that there is a meaning to life but to dare to challenge it. And whenever we wish to offer first aid in a case of existential vacuum, we should start from this conviction. There is no need to feel ashamed of existential despair because of the assumption that it is an emotional disease, for it is not a neurotic symptom but a human achievement and accomplishment. Above all, it is a manifestation of intellectual sincerity and honesty.

However, if a young man confesses to his prerogative and challenges life's meaning, he must have patience—enough patience to wait until meaning dawns upon him.

How it is possible in such cases to bring relief by having the patient view the matter objectively is shown by the following account taken from a tape-recorded dialogue with a patient who was twenty-five years of age. For several years he had been suffering from states of anxiety. Throughout the last three years he had been under psychoanalytic treatment. Now he was seeking help at the outpatient ward of the Neurological Department of the Poliklinik Hospital, and after one of the doctors on my staff had presented him to me, he told me that life often seemed to lack any meaning. He suffered from a recurrent dream in which this experience of life's total meaninglessness manifested itself. In these dreams, he would find himself among people whom he urgently asked for a solution of his problem, for liberation from this situation. He would beg them to free him from the anxiety that his life was in vain. But they would just continue to enjoy their lives, to enjoy meals, to enjoy sunshine, or whatever life had to offer them.

When he had described this dream to me, the following dialogue took place:

Frankl: That is to say, they enjoy life in a wholly unreflective manner?

Patient: Right! While I am crippled by my doubts as to the meaning of my life.

F: And what do you try to do to help yourself?

P: Sometimes it brings me relief to hear and play music. After all, Bach, Mozart, and Haydn were deeply religious personalities, and when enjoying music, I enjoy the fact that at least its creators have been granted the good fortune to arrive at a full conviction that there is a deeper or even ultimate meaning to human existence.

F: So, even if you do not believe in such a meaning yourself, you believe at least in the great believers?

P: You are right, Doctor.

F: Well, isn't it the mission of the great leaders in religion and ethics to mediate between values and meanings on the one hand, and man on the other? Man is thus given a chance to receive out of the hands of a genius of humanness, be it Moses or Jesus, Muhammad or Buddha—he is given the chance to receive from them what he is not in each instance able to obtain by himself. You see, in the field of science our intelligence might do. With respect to our beliefs, however, we must sometimes rely on and trust in other people greater than ourselves, and adopt their visions. In his search for an ultimate meaning of being, man is basically dependent on emotional rather than merely intellectual resources, as we know; in other words, he must *trust* in an ultimate meaning of being. What is more, however, this trust must be mediated by his trust in some*one*, as we now see. But now let me ask you a question: What if music touches you down to the depth of your being and moves you to tears, as is certainly the case at some moments, isn't it?—do you then, too, doubt the meaning of your life, or do you not even question it at these moments?

P: This problem then does not come to my mind at all.

F: Right. But isn't it conceivable that precisely at such moments, when you are in immediate touch with ultimate beauty, you have found the meaning of life, found it on emotional grounds without having sought for it on intellectual ones? At such moments we do not ask ourselves whether life has a meaning or not; but if we did, we could not but shout out of the depth of our existence a triumphant "yes" to being. Life, we would feel, would be worthwhile even if only lived for the sake of this unique experience.

P: I understand and agree; there are certainly moments in my life at which I do not reflect at all, and just then, meaning simply is there. I even experience a kind of union with being, and one could say as well that this is akin to the experience of being close to God as it has been reported by the great mystics.

F: Anyway, one could say that you then feel close to truth, and we are certainly justified in assuming that truth is an aspect of Deity also. Just look above my head: on the wall behind my seat you will see the shield of Harvard University, and inscribed thereon you will read *veritas*, which means truth; but as you also notice, this word is divided into three syllables which are distributed over three books, and we may well interpret this by saying that the total truth is not a universal truth, for it is not accessible to everyone. Man has rather to be satisfied with getting hold of one single aspect of the whole truth. So much more is this true of God, of whom truth is in turn no more than merely an aspect.

P: What intrigues me, however, is the question of what I should do when I feel haunted by the experience of emptiness, void of any values and meanings, and even alienated from both artistic beauty and scientific truth.

F: Well, I would say that you should not cling only to those great spirits who have found meaning but also turn to those who have sought for it in vain. You should study the writings of those philosophers who, like the French existentialists Jean-Paul Sartre and the late Albert Camus, have seemingly suffered from the same doubts that you do but have made them into a philosophy, albeit a nihilistic one. You will put your problems on an academic level, as it were, and put a distance between them and yourself. What has beset you is now seen in the light of one or another paragraph on a certain page in a given volume of one or the other author. You will recognize that to suffer from these problems is something human, even honest, an achievement and accomplishment rather than a neurotic symptom. Anyway, you will find that there is nothing to be ashamed of, but rather something to be proud of, namely, intellectual honesty. Rather than interpreting your problem in terms of a symptom, you will learn to understand it as an essential aspect of *la condition humaine* to which you then confess. You will regard yourself a member of an invisible community, the community of suffering humans, suffering from that abysmal experience of a basic meaninglessness of human existence, and at the same time struggling for a solution to the age-old problems of mankind. The same suffering and the same struggling unites you, in fact, with the best exemplars of humanity. So try to be patient and courageous: patient in leaving the problems unresolved for the time being, and courageous in not giving up the struggle for their final solution.

P: So you don't think, Doctor, that my condition is just a neurosis to overcome?

F: If a neurosis at all, I would say it is simply the collective neurosis of our day, and one that could be cured only on a collective level. Viewed in this manner, your suffering stands for that suffering which afflicts mankind as a whole, at least in the most sensitive and open-minded representatives; it is their suffering which you are shouldering!

P: And I don't mind suffering, but it should have a meaning.

F: Neither your quest for meaning nor questioning the meaning of your life is pathological. It is rather a prerogative of youth. A truly young man never takes the meaning of his life for granted but dares to challenge it. What I want to say is that you need not despair because of your despair. You should rather take this despair as evidence of the existence of what I am used to calling "the will to meaning." And in a sense, the very fact of your will to meaning justifies your faith in meaning. Or, as the famous Austrian novelist Franz Werfel once said, "Thirst is the surest proof for the existence of water." He meant, how could a man experience thirst unless water were in the world. And do not forget the words of Blaise Pascal which read: "*Le coeur a ses raisons, que la raison ne connaît point.*" [The heart has reasons which are unknown to reason.] I should say your heart has believed in an ultimate *raison d'être* all along. Sometimes the wisdom of our hearts proves to be deeper than the insight of our brains. And sometimes the most reasonable thing is not to try to be too reasonable.

P: This is precisely what I have found by myself: Sometimes in order to get relief I need only to turn to the immediate tasks confronting me.

At the outset I stated that sexual pleasure may function as an escape from existential frustration. In those cases in which the will to meaning is frustrated, the will to pleasure is not only a derivative of the will to meaning but also a substitute for it. The will to power serves an analogous and parallel purpose. Only if one's original concern with meaning fulfillment is frustrated is one either intent on pleasure, or content with power.

One of the forms the will to power takes is what I call the will to money. The will to money accounts for much of that professional overactivity which, along with sexual overactivity, functions as an escape from the awareness of an existential vacuum.

Once the will to money takes over, the pursuit of meaning is replaced by the pursuit of means. Money, instead of remaining a means, becomes an end. It ceases to serve a purpose.

What then is the meaning of money, or for that matter the meaning of possessing money? Most of those people who possess it are really possessed by it, obsessed by the urge to multiply it, and thus they nullify its meaning. For the possession of money should mean that one is in a fortunate position. One can afford to pay no attention to money, the means, but rather, to pursue the ends themselves—those ends that money should serve.

The president of an American university once offered me nine thousand dollars to join his faculty for a few weeks. He could not understand my refusal. "You want more?" he asked. "Not at all," I answered, "but if I pondered how to invest the nine thousand dollars I should say that there is one worthwhile way only in which to invest it, and that is to buy time for work. But I now have time for work, so why should I sell it for nine thousand dollars?"

Money is no end in itself. If a dollar can serve more meaning and purpose in the hands of anyone else I must not keep it in my own pocketbook. This has nothing to do with altruism. Altruism versus egoism is an obsolete alternative. As I have said, the moralistic approach to values must give way to an ontological one along whose lines good and bad are defined in terms of what promotes or blocks the fulfillment of meaning, regardless of whether it is the meaning of my self or that of someone else.

To those people who are anxious to have money as though it were an end in itself, "time is money." They exhibit a need for speed. To them, driving a fast car becomes an end in itself. This is a defense mechanism, an attempt to escape the confrontation with an existential vacuum. The less one is aware of a goal the faster he tries to cover the road. The famous Viennese comedian Qualtinger, playing the part of a hooligan, sat on a motorcycle and sang, "It is true, I have no idea where I am going, but anyway, I am getting there faster."

This is an example of what I would call centrifugal leisure as opposed to centripetal leisure. Today centrifugal leisure is predominant. Flight from the self allows for avoiding a confrontation with the void in the self. Centripetal leisure would allow for solving problems—and to begin with, facing them. People vacillating between professional overactivity and centrifugal leisure have no time to finish their thoughts. When they begin to think, a secretary comes in and asks for a signature, or a telephone call must be answered. What then happens has been described by the psalmist. *"Vel per noctem me monet cor meum."* Even at night his heart admonishes him. Today he would say that at night the repressed existential problems return. Conscience reminds him of them. This is the origin of what I would call noogenic sleeplessness. People suffering from it often take sleeping pills. They fall asleep, it is true, but they also fall prey to the pathogenic effect of repression. Not repression of the sexual facts of life, but repression of the existential facts of life.

We need new types of leisure which allow for contemplation and meditation. To this end, man needs the courage to be lonely.

In the final analysis the existential vacuum is a paradox. If we only broadened our horizon we would notice that we enjoy our freedom, but we are not yet fully aware of our responsibility. If we were, we would realize that there is plenty of meaning waiting to be fulfilled by us, be it with respect to underprivileged people or with respect to underdeveloped countries.

To be sure, we would have to begin by amplifying our concept of the oneness of man. What is at stake is not only the oneness of man but also the oneness of mankind.

Thousands of years ago mankind developed monotheism. Today another step is due. I would call it monanthropism. Not the belief in the one God but rather the awareness of the one mankind, the awareness of the unity of humanity; a unity in whose light the different colors of our skins would fade away.[13]

[13] I am in no way against discrimination. To be sure, I am not for racial but rather for radical discrimination. That is to say, I am for judging each individual on the grounds of the unique "race" that is represented by him alone. In other words, I am for personal rather than racial discrimination.

LOGOTHERAPEUTIC

TECHNIQUES

✹ ✹ ✹ IN cases of noogenic neurosis, logotherapy is a specific therapy. In other words, what a patient caught in the existential despair over the apparent meaninglessness of his life needs is logotherapy rather than psychotherapy. This, however, is not true of the psychogenic neuroses. Here logotherapy cannot be opposed to psychotherapy but itself represents one among the schools of psychotherapy.

Let us now discuss how logotherapy may be applied in psychogenic cases, although an adequate introduction to its clinical applications must be based on case material and should presuppose a hospital setting. As compared with training through case presentations and discussions, even training analyses are relatively unimportant.

The clinical applications of logotherapy really follow from its anthropological implications. The logotherapeutic techniques called dereflection and paradoxical intention both rest on two essential qualities of human existence, namely, man's capacities of self-transcendence and self-detachment.[1]

When discussing the motivational theory of logotherapy I pointed out that the direct intention of pleasure defeats itself.

[1] Viktor E. Frankl, "Logotherapy and Existential Analysis—A Review," *American Journal of Psychotherapy* 20: 252, 1966.

The more an individual aims at pleasure the more he misses the aim. In logotherapy we speak in this context of hyper-intention. Along with this pathogenic phenomenon we may observe another one, which in logotherapy is called hyper-reflection. Hyperreflection means excessive attention.

There is also a phenomenon that may justifiably be called mass hyperreflection. It is particularly observable within the culture of the United States where many people are intent always to watch themselves, to analyze themselves as to the alleged hidden motivations of their behavior, to interpret this behavior in terms of the unconscious psychodynamics under-lying it. Professor Edith Weisskopf-Joelson of the University of Georgia has found that among American students self-inter-pretation and, next to it, self-actualization are regarded as the highest values—statistically significantly higher than any others. Growing up in such a climate, people are often haunted by a fatalistic expectation of the crippling effects of their pasts so they actually become crippled. A reader of one of my books once wrote a letter to me and made the following confession: "I have suffered more from the thought that I should have complexes than from actually having them. Actually, I wouldn't trade my experiences for anything and believe a lot of good came out of them."

Spontaneity and activity are impeded if made a target of too much attention. Consider the centipede who, as a story has it, was asked by his enemy in what sequence he moved his legs. When the centipede paid attention to the problem, he was unable to move his legs at all. He is said to have died from starvation. Should we say that he died from fatal hyper-reflection?

In logotherapy hyperreflection is counteracted by dereflec-tion. One of those domains in which this technique is applied is that of sexual neuroses, whether frigidity or impotence. Sexual performance or experience is strangled to the extent to which it is made either an object of attention or an objective of intention.[2] In cases of impotence, the patient frequently approaches sexual intercourse as something which is demanded of him. I have elaborated on this aspect of the etiology of impotence elsewhere.[3] A logotherapeutic technique has been developed to remove the demand quality the patient attaches to sexual intercourse.[4] The logotherapeutic treatment of sexual neurosis is applicable regardless of whether or not one adopts the logotherapeutic theory. In the Neurological Department of the Poliklinik Hospital in Vienna, I have entrusted an outpatient ward for patients with sexual neuroses to a doctor who is a strict Freudian, but in the given setting, where only short-term procedures are indicated, he uses the logotherapeutic rather than the psychoanalytic technique.

Whereas dereflection is part of the logotherapeutic treatment of sexual neurosis, paradoxical intention lends itself to the short-term treatment of obsessive-compulsive and phobic patients.[5]

[2] As far as frigidity is concerned, the reader is referred to an instructive and illustrative case I have included in my book, *Man's Search for Meaning: An Introduction to Logotherapy,* Washington Square Press, New York, 1963, pp. 194 f.

[3] Viktor E. Frankl, *The Doctor and the Soul: From Psychotherapy to Logotherapy,* second, expanded edition, Alfred A. Knopf, New York, 1965, pp. 159 ff.

[4] I have discussed this technique in the opening paper before the Symposium on Logotherapy in the framework of the International Congress of Psychotherapy in London (Viktor E. Frankl, "Logotherapy and Existential Analysis—A Review," *American Journal of Psychotherapy* 20: 252, 1966).

[5] In German I described paradoxical intention as early as 1939 in a paper ("Zur medikamentösen Unterstützung der Psychotherapie bei Neurosen," *Schweizer Archiv für Neurologie und Psychiatrie* 43: 26-31); in English I described it in 1955 in my book, *The Doctor and the*

Paradoxical intention means that the patient is encouraged to do, or wish to happen, the very things he fears. In order to understand the therapeutic efficiency of this technique we must consider the phenomenon called "anticipatory anxiety." By this I mean that the patient reacts to an event with a fearful expectation of its recurrence. However, fear tends to make happen precisely that which one fears, and so does anticipatory anxiety. Thus a vicious circle is established. A symptom evokes a phobia and the phobia provokes the symptom. The recurrence of the symptom then reinforces the phobia. The patient is caught in a cocoon. A feedback mechanism is established.

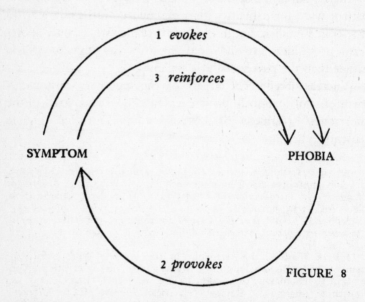

FIGURE 8

Soul: An Introduction to Logotherapy (Alfred A. Knopf, New York), and elaborated on it in a paper ("Paradoxical Intention: A Logotherapeutic Technique," *American Journal of Psychotherapy* 14: 520, 1960) which has been reprinted in another of my books (*Psychotherapy and Existentialism: Selected Papers on Logotherapy*, Washington Square Press, New York, 1967).

How can we break up the vicious circle? It can be managed either by pharmacotherapy or by psychotherapy, or by a combination of the two. This last is necessary in severe cases.[6]

Pharmacotherapy is the best way to begin in those cases with agoraphobic symptoms in which hyperthyroidism is an underlying factor,[7] or those cases of claustrophobia which can be traced to latent tetany.[8] One should bear in mind, however, that the organic factor involved in such cases provides no more than a mere inclination to anxiety, while the full-fledged anxiety neurosis does not develop unless the anticipatory anxiety mechanism comes into play. Therefore, to unhinge the circle one must attack it on the psychic pole as well as on the organic pole. And the first is precisely the job done by paradoxical intention.

What then is going on when paradoxical intention is applied? Encouraging the patient to do, or wish to happen, the very things he fears engenders an inversion of intention. The pathogenic fear is replaced by a paradoxical wish. By the same token, however, the wind is taken out of the sails of anticipatory anxiety.

I have spoken of an inversion of intention. What then is the intention on the part of a phobic individual? The intention is to avoid those situations which arouse anxiety. In logotherapy, we speak of flight from fear. We may observe it in those cases,

---

[6] Such as those which I have described in the chapter on paradoxical intention of my book, *The Doctor and the Soul*, pp. 248 ff.

[7] Viktor E. Frankl, "Psychische Symptome und neurotische Reaktionen bei Hyperthyreose," *Medizinische Klinik* 51: 1139, 1956.

[8] The physiological origin of these conditions has been demonstrated in my own research in my department at the Vienna Poliklinik Hospital. Incidentally, the first tranquilizer ever developed on the Continent—it was developed by me as early as 1952 (Viktor E. Frankl, "Zur Behandlung der Angst," *Wiener medizinische Wochenschrift* 102: 535, 1952)—even lends itself to the drug treatment of these claustrophobias in a special way (Viktor E. Frankl, "Über somatogene Pseudoneurosen," *Wiener Klinische Wochenschrift* 68: 280, 1956).

for example, in which anxiety itself is the target of fear—in which the patient himself speaks of "fear of fear." He really fears the potential effects of fear, be it a faint, a coronary attack, or a stroke.

According to logotherapeutic teachings, flight from fear is a pathogenic pattern.[9] More specifically it is the phobic pattern. *But the development of a phobia can be obviated by confronting one with the situation he begins to fear.* In order to illustrate the point, I would like to recount an experience of my own. During a rock climb in foggy and rainy weather, I saw a fellow climber fall. Although he was found about six hundred feet below the spot, he survived the accident. Two weeks later I scaled the same trail up the steep wall of the mountain. As it happened the weather was again foggy and rainy. However, despite the psychic shock I had suffered, I defied the situation and by so doing overcame the psychic trauma.

Alongside flight from fear there are two more pathogenic patterns, namely, fight for pleasure and fight against obsessions and compulsions. Fight for pleasure is identical with hyperintention of pleasure, that is to say, one of the major factors underlying sexual neuroses. Fight against obsessions and compulsions is the pathogenic pattern underlying obsessive-compulsive neuroses. Obsessive-compulsive neurotics are plagued by the idea that they might commit suicide or even homicide or that the strange thoughts which haunt them might be signs of imminent, if not present, psychosis. In other words, they fear the potential effects or the potential cause of the strange thoughts. The phobic pattern of flight from fear is paralleled by the obsessive-compulsive pattern. Obsessive-compulsive neurotics also display fear. But theirs is not "fear of fear" but rather fear of themselves, and their response

[9] Viktor E. Frankl, "Angst und Zwang. Zur Kenntnis pathogener Reaktionsmuster," *Acta Psychotherapeutica* 1: 111, 1953.

is to fight against obsessions and compulsions. But the more the patients fight, the stronger their symptoms become. In other words, alongside the circle formation built up by anticipatory anxiety in phobic cases, there is another feedback mechanism which we may encounter in the obsessive-compulsive neurotic. Pressure induces counter-pressure, and counter-pressure, in turn, increases pressure. If one succeeds in making the patient stop fighting his obsessions and compulsions—and this may well be accomplished by paradoxical intention—these symptoms soon diminish and finally atrophy.

Having discussed the theory let us turn to the practice of paradoxical intention. Let us take up a case report. Edith Weisskopf-Joelson,[10] of the Department of Psychology at the University of Georgia, makes the following statement:

"I have made use of 'paradoxical intention' with many of my patients, including myself, and I have found it very effective. For example, a university student complained about being anxious with regard to an oral report to be given—let us say—on Friday. I advised him to take his appointment calendar and to write on every page of the week, with large letters, the word 'ANXIETY.' As it were—I asked him to plan for an anxious week. He was much relieved after doing this because now he was suffering from anxiety only, but not from anxiety about anxiety."

Another instance of paradoxical intention is the following:

The patient refused to leave his house because every time he did he had attacks of fear that he would collapse on the street. Every time he did leave his house he returned after a few steps. He ran away from his fear. He was admitted to my department at the Poliklinik. My staff gave him a thorough checkup and made certain that there was nothing wrong with

[10] Edith Weisskopf-Joelson, "The Present Crisis in Psychotherapy," *The Journal of Psychology* 69: 107–115, 1968.

his heart. One of the doctors told him that. Then he suggested the patient should go out on the street and try to get a heart attack. The doctor told him, "Tell yourself that yesterday you had two heart attacks, and today you have time to get three—it's still early in the morning. Tell yourself that you will have a nice, fat coronary, and a stroke to boot." For the first time the patient was able to break through the cocoon in which he had enclosed himself.

There is evidence that paradoxical intention even works in chronic cases.[11] For example, in the *German Encyclopaedia of Psychotherapy*,[12] there is a case study of a sixty-five-year-old woman who suffered from a hand-washing compulsion for sixty years. A member of my staff successfully applied the paradoxical intention technique in this case.

In the *American Journal of Psychotherapy*, Ralph G. Victor and Carolyn M. Krug[13] of the Department of Psychiatry at the University of Washington in Seattle published the report of a case in which they had ventured to apply the technique of paradoxical intention to compulsive gambling. The patient, who was thirty-six years old, had been gambling since the age of fourteen. After he had been instructed to gamble daily during three specified hours, the patient observed that he "had the deep feeling that after twenty years and five psychiatrists, this was the first time a *creative* approach had been taken to

[11] H. O. Gerz, "The Treatment of the Phobic and the Obsessive-Compulsive Patient Using Paradoxical Intention Sec. Viktor E. Frankl," *Journal of Neuropsychiatry* 3: 375, 1962.

[12] K. Kocourek, E. Niebauer, and P. Polak, "Ergebnisse der klinischen Anwendung der Logotherapie," in *Handbuch der Neurosenlehre und Psychotherapie*, edited by V. E. Frankl, V. E. von Gebsattel, and J. H. Schultz, Urban & Schwarzenberg, Munich-Berlin, 1959, Vol. 3, p. 752.

[13] Ralph G. Victor and Carolyn M. Krug, "Paradoxical Intention in the Treatment of Compulsive Gambling," *American Journal of Psychotherapy* 21: 808, 1967.

the problem." The patient lost, and within three weeks was completely out of cash. But "the therapist suggested that he might sell his watch." As a matter of fact, "following treatment by paradoxical intention, that patient for the first time in more than twenty years gained a remission."

J. Lehembre has tried paradoxical intention on children at the Dutch universities of Utrecht and Nijmegen, in the departments of Psychiatry and Pediatrics, respectively. He has been successful in most cases. In his report, published in the *Acta Neurologica et Psychiatrica Belgica*,[14] he makes the point that only in a single case has symptom substitution been observed.

In the USSR, paradoxical intention, according to a statement made by Professor A. M. Swjadostsch, is being used in his "hospital with success in the treatment of phobias and anticipatory anxiety neuroses" (personal communication).

Jaspers' dictum "in philosophy, being new speaks against being true" may also hold for psychotherapy. Unwillingly and unwittingly, paradoxical intention has always existed. An example of unwilling use was reported to me by the head of the Department of Psychiatry at the University of Mainz in West Germany. When he was in junior high school his class was to present a play. One of the characters was a stutterer, so they gave this role to a student who actually stuttered. Soon, however, he had to give up the role because it turned out that when standing on the stage he was completely unable to stutter. He had to be replaced by another boy.

With regard to unwitting use, an instance of paradoxical intention is the following:

One of my American students, who had to take his exams

14 J. Lehembre, "L'intention paradoxale, procédé de psychothérapie," *Acta Neurologica et Psychiatrica Belgica* 64: 725, 1964.

from me and in this setting was to explain paradoxical intention, resorted to the following autobiographical account: "My stomach used to growl in company of others. The more I tried to keep it from happening, the more it growled. Soon I started to take it for granted that it would be with me the rest of my life. Began to live with it—laughed with others about it. Soon it disappeared."

In this context, I should like to place emphasis on the fact that my student adopted a humorous attitude toward a symptom. In fact, paradoxical intention should always be formulated in as humorous a manner as possible. Humor is indeed a definitely human phenomenon.[15] After all, no beast is capable of laughing. What is even more important, humor allows man to create perspective, to put distance between himself and whatever may confront him. By the same token, humor allows man to detach himself from himself and thereby to attain the fullest possible control over himself. To make use of the human capacity of self-detachment is what paradoxical intention basically achieves. Keeping this in mind, it seems no longer true "that we do not as yet take humor seriously enough," as Konrad Lorenz[16] contends in his most recent book.

On the subject of humor, Gordon W. Allport raised an important question after I had read a paper at Harvard University. The question was whether or not that sound sense of

[15] Speaking of humor, I am justified in defining paradoxical intention in terms of a joke: A boy who came to school late offered as an excuse to the teacher the fact that the icy streets were so slippery that whenever he moved one step forward he slipped two steps back again. Thereupon the teacher retorted: "But now I have caught you in a lie— if this had been true, you never could have succeeded in arriving at school." Whereupon the boy calmly replied: "Why not? I just turned around and headed for home." Wasn't this paradoxical intention? Wasn't the boy successful through an inversion of the original intention?

[16] Konrad Lorenz, *On Aggression*, Bantam Books, New York, 1967, p. 284.

humor which is inherent in the technique of paradoxical intention is equally available in all patients. I replied that in principle each and every human being, by virtue of his humanness, is capable of detaching himself from himself and laughing about himself. But there are certainly quantitative differences in the degree to which the human capacity for self-detachment and the sound sense of humor can be mobilized. An example of a low degree is the following:

I had a man in my department, a guard in a museum who could not stay on his job because he suffered from deadly fears that someone would steal a painting. During a round I made with my staff, I tried paradoxical intention with him: "Tell yourself they stole a Rembrandt yesterday and today they will steal a Rembrandt and a Van Gogh." He just stared at me and said, "But, Herr Professor, that's against the law!" This man simply was too feeble-minded to understand the meaning of paradoxical intention.

In this respect paradoxical intention, or for that matter logotherapy, is not an exception. It is the rule that psychotherapy—every method of psychotherapy, that is—is not applicable to every patient with the same degree of success. Moreover, not every doctor is capable of handling every method of psychotherapy with the same degree of skill. The method of choice in a given case is like an equation with two unknowns:

$$\psi = x + y$$

The first unknown represents the unique personality of the patient. The second unknown represents the unique personality of the doctor. Both have to be taken into account before a method of psychotherapy is chosen. What holds for other methods of psychotherapy is also true of logotherapy.

Logotherapy is no panacea, nor, for that matter, is any other psychotherapy a panacea. A psychoanalyst once said of his kind of therapy: "This technique has proved to be the only method suited to my individuality; I do not venture to deny that a physician quite differently constituted might feel impelled to adopt a different attitude to his patients and the task before him." The man who made this confession was Sigmund Freud.

Since logotherapy is no panacea, there can be no objection to combining it with other methods, as such psychiatrists as Ledermann (hypnosis),[17] Bazzi (relaxation training after Schultz),[18] Kvilhaug (behavior therapy),[19] Vorbusch,[20] and Gerz (pharmacotherapy)[21] have suggested.

On the other hand, the remarkable results obtained by paradoxical intention cannot be explained merely in terms of suggestion. Actually, our patients often set out to use paradoxical intention with a strong conviction that it simply cannot work and yet they finally succeed. In other words, they succeed not because of, but rather in spite of suggestion. Benedikt[22] subjected his patients to test batteries in order to evaluate their susceptibility to suggestion. The patients proved less suscep-

[17] F. K. Ledermann, "Clinical Applications of Existential Psychotherapy," *Journal of Existential Psychiatry* 3: 45, 1962.

[18] T. Bazzi, Paper read before the International Congress of Psychotherapy, Barcelona, 1958.

[19] B. Kvilhaug, "Klinische Erfahrungen mit der logotherapeutischen Technik der paradoxen Intention beziehungsweise deren Kombination mit anderen Behandlungsmethoden (Bericht über 40 Fälle)," Paper read before the Austrian Medical Society of Psychotherapy, Vienna, July 18, 1963.

[20] H. J. Vorbusch, "Die Behandlung schwerer Schlafstorungen mit der paradoxen Intention," Paper read before the Austrian Medical Society of Psychotherapy, Vienna, June 1, 1965.

[21] H. O. Gerz, "Severe Depressive and Anxiety States," *Mind* 1: 235, 1963.

[22] Fritz Benedikt, "Zur Therapie angst- und zwangsneurotischer Symptome mit Hilfe der 'Paradoxen Intention' und 'Dereflexion' nach V. E. Frankl," Dissertation, University of Munich Medical School, 1966.

tible to suggestion than the average, but paradoxical intention was successful in their cases.

Gerz,[23, 24] Lebzeltern, and Tweedie[25, 26] have proved that paradoxical intention must not be confounded with persuasion. However, it is my contention that in some cases paradoxical intention cannot be launched without being preceded by persuasion. That is particularly true of obsessions with blasphemy, for the treatment of which a special logotherapeutic technique has been devised.[27]

Most of the authors who have practiced paradoxical intention and published their work agree that it is a short-term procedure. However, as Emil A. Gutheil,[28] the late editor of the *American Journal of Psychotherapy*, wrote, "[The assumption] that the durability of results corresponds to the length of therapy [is one of] the illusions of Freudian orthodoxy." And as J. H. Schultz,[29] the grand old man of German psychotherapy, wrote, it is "a completely baseless assertion that symptom removal must be followed by substitute symptoms." Edith

[23] H. O. Gerz, "The Treatment of the Phobic and the Obsessive-Compulsive Patient Using Paradoxical Intention Sec. Viktor E. Frankl," *Journal of Neuropsychiatry* 3: 375, 1962.

[24] H. O. Gerz, "Experience with the Logotherapeutic Technique of Paradoxical Intention in the Treatment of Phobic and Obsessive-Compulsive Patients," Paper read before the Symposium on Logotherapy at the Sixth International Congress of Psychotherapy, London, 1964. *American Journal of Psychiatry* 123: 548, 1966.

[25] D. F. Tweedie, *Logotherapy and the Christian Faith: An Evaluation of Frankl's Existential Approach to Psychotherapy*, Baker Book House, Grand Rapids, Michigan, 1961.

[26] D. F. Tweedie, *The Christian and the Couch: An Introduction to Christian Logotherapy*, Baker Book House, Grand Rapids, Michigan, 1963.

[27] Viktor E. Frankl, *The Doctor and the Soul: From Psychotherapy to Logotherapy*, Alfred A. Knopf, New York, 1965, p. 239.

[28] E. A. Gutheil, "Proceedings of the Association for the Advancement of Psychotherapy," *American Journal of Psychotherapy* 10: 134, 1956.

[29] J. H. Schultz, "Analytische und organismische Psychotherapie," *Acta Psychotherapeutica* 1: 33, 1953.

Weisskopf-Joelson,[30, 31] who is a psychoanalyst, has expressed the same view in a paper on logotherapy. "Psychoanalytically oriented therapists," she says, "might argue that no real improvement can be achieved with methods such as logotherapy, since the pathology in 'deeper' layers remains untouched, while the therapist limits himself to the strengthening or erecting of defenses. Such conclusions are not free of danger. They may keep us from the awareness of major sources of mental health because these sources do not fit into a specific theoretical framework. We must not forget that such concepts as 'defenses,' 'deeper layers,' and 'adequate functioning on a superficial level with underlying pathology' are theoretical concepts rather than empirical observations." By contrast, the results obtained by paradoxical intention do deserve to be qualified as empirical observations.

Another psychoanalyst, Glenn G. Golloway of the Ypsilanti State Hospital, contends that paradoxical intention does not resolve the "underlying conflict." But, he says, this "does not detract from paradoxical intention as a successful technique. It is no insult to surgery that it does not cure the diseased gallbladder it removes. The patient is better off."

"What then does paradoxical intention do," is the question Leston L. Havens[32] of Harvard Medical School's Department of Psychiatry has asked himself, and answered "in the familiar language," i.e., in psychodynamic terms: "The patient is told to discharge the forbidden impulse; he is given permission. More specifically, his inhibitions are dismissed. . . . Surely what Frankl is recommending falls under the old term 'superego

[30] Edith Weisskopf-Joelson, "Some Comments on a Viennese School of Psychiatry," *Journal of Abnormal and Social Psychology* 51: 701, 1955.
[31] Edith Weisskopf-Joelson, "Logotherapy and Existential Analysis," *Acta Psychotherapeutica* 17: 554, 1963.
[32] Leston L. Havens, "Paradoxical Intention," *Psychiatry & Social Science Review*, 2: 2, 1968, pp. 16–19.

modification.' . . . The doctor intervenes to supply the patient with a more permissive conscience. What is affected are the patient's standards and ideals. For the patient lacking ideals, Frankl helps him find new ones. For the symptomatic patient suffering from his punitive ideals, Frankl attempts to modify them."

For this reason many psychoanalysts have been using the paradoxical intention technique successfully. Some workers in the field try to explain this success in psychodynamic terms.[33] Others, such as D. Müller-Hegemann,[34] described paradoxical intention as a "neurophysiologically oriented approach." He writes that he has "observed favorable results in the last years in patients suffering from phobias and therefore considers paradoxical intention to have much merit." Again, it should be noted that even doctors who adhere to theories different from the one which underlies logotherapy include paradoxical intention in their armamentarium.

Attempts have been made to clarify the indications for logotherapy. For example, Gerz, clinical director of the Connecticut Valley Hospital, feels that paradoxical intention is a specific and effective treatment of phobic and obsessive-compulsive conditions. It "lends itself in acute cases to short-term therapy."[35]

[33] Viktor E. Frankl, *Psychotherapy and Existentialism: Selected Papers on Logotherapy,* Washington Square Press, New York, 1967; H. O. Gerz, "The Treatment of the Phobic and the Obsessive-Compulsive Patient Using Paradoxical Intention Sec. Viktor E. Frankl," *Journal of Neuropsychiatry* 3: 375, 1962.

[34] The director of the Neuropsychiatric Clinic of Karl Marx University in Leipzig, East Germany. See his article, "Methodological Approaches in Psychotherapy," *American Journal of Psychotherapy* 17: 554, 1963.

[35] H. O. Gerz, "Experience with the Logotherapeutic Technique of Paradoxical Intention in the Treatment of Phobic and Obsessive-Compulsive Patients," Paper read before the Symposium on Logotherapy at the Sixth International Congress of Psychotherapy, London, 1964. *American Journal of Psychiatry* 123: 548, 1966.

With respect to statistics Gerz reported: ". . . 88.2 percent of all patients recovered or made considerable improvement. Most of these cases suffered from their illness up to 24 years . . . Those who have been sick for several years need up to 12 months of biweekly sessions to bring about recovery. Most acute cases who are sick for a few weeks or months respond to paradoxical intention within about 4 to 12 sessions."[36]

Dr. Gerz adds: ". . . it is understandable that the psychiatrist with many years of psychoanalytic training might tend to be prejudiced and to reject paradoxical intention without having tried it."[37] And, no doubt, much of the resistance to paradoxical intention, and for that matter to logotherapy, stems from emotional grounds such as loyalty and obedience to a sect. But the sectarian should bear in mind Freud's own admonition that "reverence before the greatness of a genius is certainly a great thing. But our reverence before facts should exceed it."[38]

Important as it is to determine the indications for logotherapy and paradoxical intention, it is even more important to determine contraindications. Paradoxical intention is strictly contraindicated in psychotic depressions. For such patients a special logotherapeutic technique is reserved whose guiding principle is the decrease of the guilt feelings the patient suffers because of his tendency to self-accusations.[39] It would be a misconception of existential psychiatry to interpret these self-accusations as indicating that the patient really is guilty, "exis-

[36] H. O. Gerz, "The Treatment of the Phobic and the Obsessive-Compulsive Patient Using Paradoxical Intention Sec. Viktor E. Frankl," *Journal of Neuropsychiatry* 3: 375, 1962.

[37] *Ibid.*

[38] Sigmund Freud, "Book Review," *Wiener medizinische Wochenschrift,* 1889.

[39] Viktor E. Frankl, *The Doctor and the Soul: From Psychotherapy to Logotherapy,* second, expanded edition, Alfred A. Knopf, New York, 1965, pp. 261 ff.

tentially guilty," and hence depressed. This would amount to mistaking an effect for the cause. Moreover, such an interpretation would reinforce the patient's guilt feelings to an extent that might well result in his suicide. Incidentally, logotherapy offers a special test to evaluate the suicide risk in a given case.[40]

As far as schizophrenic patients are concerned, logotherapy is far from providing a causal treatment. As a psychotherapeutic adjunct, however, the logotherapeutic technique called dereflection is recommended for such patients (see page 126).[41] The volume, *Modern Psychotherapeutic Practice*,[42] includes some tape-recorded sessions with schizophrenic patients to demonstrate the use of dereflection.

Burton[43] recently stated that "the last 50 years of therapeutic psychiatry have made a fetish of the deep personal history of the patient. Freud's startling cures of supposed unremitting hysterias led us to seek a similar traumatic experience in every patient and to reify insight as curative, something we are only now recovering from." But even if one assumes that neuroses or even psychoses are caused by what is supposed to cause them in terms of psychodynamic hypotheses, logotherapy would still be indicated in terms of a noncausal treatment.[44] As long as there is an existential vacuum in the patient, the symptoms will rush into it. That is why the "logotherapeutic

[40] *Ibid.*

[41] *Ibid.*, p. 260, pp. 264 ff.

[42] Viktor E. Frankl, "Fragments from the Logotherapeutic Treatment of Four Cases," in *Modern Psychotherapeutic Practice: Innovations in Technique*, edited by Arthur Burton, Science and Behavior Books, Palo Alto, California, 1965.

[43] Arthur Burton, "Beyond Transference," *Psychotherapy: Theory, Research and Practice* 1: 49, 1964.

[44] Edith Weisskopf-Joelson, "Some Comments on a Viennese School of Psychiatry," *Journal of Abnormal and Social Psychology* 51: 701, 1955; "Logotherapy and Existential Analysis," *Acta Psychotherapeutica* 17: 554, 1963.

encounter," as Crumbaugh[45] contends, "continues beyond where most therapies, especially analytically oriented methods, stop: it holds that unless purposeful goals and commitment to them is attained, therapy will have been for naught, as the pathological etiology will remain and the symptom will later return."

Some authors[46] contend that in existential psychiatry, logotherapy is the only school which has evolved psychotherapeutic techniques. Even more, it has been said that logotherapy adds a new dimension to psychotherapy: that it adds to it the dimension of the distinctively human phenomena. In fact, two specifically human phenomena, the capacity of self-transcendence and the capacity of self-detachment, are mobilized by the logotherapeutic techniques of dereflection and paradoxical intention, respectively. Professor Petrilowitsch of the Department of Psychiatry at the University of Mainz, West Germany, ascribes the surprising results obtained by these two logotherapeutic techniques to the fact that logotherapy does not remain in the dimension of neurosis, that is, in the dimension of dynamics or conditioning processes. In contrast to behavior therapy, for example, logotherapy is not satisfied with reconditioning but opens the dimension of the very humanness of man and draws upon the resources which are available in the *humanitas* of the *homo patiens*.

This might be what Paul E. Johnson[47] had in mind when he said that "logotherapy is not a rival therapy against others, but it may well be a challenge to them in its plus factor."

[45] J. C. Crumbaugh, "The Application of Logotherapy," *Journal of Existentialism* 5: 403, 1965.
[46] See, among others, Joseph Lyons, "Existential Psychotherapy: Fact, Hope, Fiction," *Journal of Abnormal and Social Psychology* 62: 242, 1961.
[47] Paul E. Johnson, "The Challenge of Logotherapy," *Journal of Religion and Health* 7: 122, 1968.

MEDICAL MINISTRY

ɤ ɤ ɤ MEDICAL ministry is that aspect within the logo-therapeutic system which deals with the treatment of somatogenic cases rather than that of noogenic or psychogenic neuroses. It goes without saying that somatogenic cases are dealt with in logotherapeutic terms only insofar as they do not yield to therapy in the strict sense, that is to say, insofar as the somatic cause of the trouble cannot be removed. What then matters is the stand a patient takes toward his predicament, the attitude he chooses toward his suffering: in other words, the fulfillment of the potential meaning of suffering. It goes without saying that we must give preference to causal treatment of disease, and resort to medical ministry only if causal treatment proves to be of no avail. Then the treatment of the patient's attitude toward his disease is the one thing possible and necessary.

It goes to the credit of Joyce Travelbee of New York University that not only a doctor's but also a nurse's responsibilities and opportunities in this respect have been explored. In a book based on the concept of logotherapy she succeeds in systematizing a methodology "designed to assist patients to arrive at meaning."[1] She writes that her "major belief is that

[1] Joyce Travelbee, *Interpersonal Aspects of Nursing*, F. A. Davis Company, Philadelphia, 1966, p. 171.

human beings are motivated by a search for meaning in all life experiences, and meaning can be found in the experience of illness, suffering and pain."[2] In order to show the lines along which Professor Travelbee proceeds, let me quote one of the methods listed by her, namely, the "parable method":[3]

"The parable method seems particularly suited for some patients. In using this particular method the nurse, during her interaction with the patient, relates a parable or tells a story which illustrates the point that no human being is exempt from illness. One particularly useful parable or story is 'The Parable of the Mustard Seed.' Gotami was born in India. She married and went to the house of her husband's people to live. She bore a son but the boy died. She began to grieve. She took her son with her from place to place asking for medicine for him. People scoffed and laughed at her. One man took pity on her and told her to seek the assistance of the foremost individual in the world. Taking her son with her she asked the great teacher for medicine for her son. The teacher told her that she had done well in coming to him for medicine. He told her to go throughout the city and, in whatever house no one had suffered or died, from that house to bring a grain of mustard seed. She went from house to house and never succeeded in finding a house where no one had suffered. She realized that her son was not the only child who suffered and that suffering was a law common to mankind."

An example of meaningful suffering drawn from my own practice is the story of the old general practitioner who consulted me because of his depression after his wife had died. Using the form of a Socratic dialogue, I asked him what would have happened if he rather than his wife had died first. "How she would have suffered," he said. I replied, "Don't you see,

[2] *Ibid.*, p. v.
[3] *Ibid.*, p. 176.

Doctor, that great suffering has been spared her, and it is you who have spared her this suffering; but now, you have to pay for it by surviving and mourning her."[4] Our dialogue induced him to discover a meaning in his suffering, the meaning of a sacrifice for the sake of his wife.

I told the story before a group in America and an American psychoanalyst made a comment that illustrated the reductionist approach to meaning and values. Here it is: "I understand your point, Dr. Frankl; however, if we start from the fact that obviously your patient had only suffered so deeply from the death of his wife because unconsciously he had hated her all along . . ." Whereupon I said: "It may well be that after having the patient lie down on your analytical couch for, say, five hundred hours, you might have succeeded in bringing him to the point where, like the Communists behind the Iron Curtain in the course of what they call self-criticism, he confesses: 'Yes, Doctor, you are right, I hated my wife all along . . .' But then you also would have deprived the patient of the only treasure he still possessed, namely, the awareness of the unique love and marital life he and his wife had built up . . ."

In a book of mine[5] I have described a logotherapeutic procedure designed to promote the discovery of meaning and values. It is the technique of the common denominator, as I have called it. According to Max Scheler, valuing means preferring a higher value to a lower one. It is my contention that it is easy to compare the ranks of values if a common denominator is perceived.

Life's transitoriness belongs to what I have called the tragic triad of human existence. Hence it is also a problem which

[4] Viktor E. Frankl, *Man's Search for Meaning: An Introduction to Logotherapy*, Washington Square Press, New York, 1963, p. 179.

[5] Viktor E. Frankl, *The Doctor and the Soul: From Psychotherapy to Logotherapy*, second, expanded edition, Alfred A. Knopf, New York, 1965, pp. 277 ff.

besets the patient with an incurable disease who confronts not only suffering but even imminent death. In such cases the question is how to convey to the patient our conviction that in the past nothing is lost, but everything is stored as though it were safely deposited in a storehouse. The past is the safest mode of being. What is past has been saved and rescued by us into the past. The volume, *Modern Psychotherapeutic Practice*,[6] includes a tape-recorded interview I had with an eighty-year-old patient. She was suffering from a cancer which could not be successfully treated. Because of this fact, which she knew, she had become depressed. I demonstrated the case to the students who attended my clinical lecture on logotherapy. Our dialogue, of which my part was sheer improvisation, went as follows:

Frankl: What do you think of when you look back on your life? Has life been worth living?

Patient: Well, Doctor, I must say that I had a good life. Life was nice, indeed. And I must thank the Lord for what it held for me: I went to theaters, I attended concerts, and so forth. You see, Doctor, I went there with the family in whose house I served for many decades as a maid, in Prague, at first, and afterward in Vienna. And for the grace of all of these wonderful experiences, I am grateful to the Lord.

(I nevertheless felt that she also was doubtful about the ultimate meaning of her life as a whole, and I wanted to steer her through her doubts. But first I had to provoke them, and then to wrestle with them—wrestle with them as Jacob did

6 Viktor E. Frankl, "Fragments from the Logotherapeutic Treatment of Four Cases," in *Modern Psychotherapeutic Practice: Innovations in Technique,* edited by Arthur Burton, Science and Behavior Books, Palo Alto, California, 1965.

with the angel until he blessed him: that is how I wanted to wrestle with my patient's repressed and unconscious existential despair so that she, too, could finally "bless" her life, say "yes" to her life in spite of everything. So my task consisted in having her question the meaning of her life on the conscious level rather than repressing her doubts.)

F: You are speaking of some wonderful experiences; but all this will have an end now, won't it?

P (*thoughtfully*): Yes, everything ends . . .

F: Well, do you think now that all the wonderful things of your life might be annihilated?

P (*still more thoughtfully*): All those wonderful things . . .

F: But tell me: do you think that anyone can undo the happiness that you have experienced? Can anyone blot it out?

P: No, Doctor, nobody can blot it out!

F: Or can anyone blot out the goodness you have met in your life?

P (*becoming increasingly emotionally involved*): Nobody can blot it out!

F: What you have achieved and accomplished—

P: Nobody can blot it out!

F: Or what you have bravely and honestly suffered: can anyone remove it from the world—remove it from the past where you have stored it, as it were?

P (*now moved to tears*): No one can remove it! (*Pause*) It is true, I have had a great deal to suffer; but I also tried to be courageous and steadfast in enduring what I must. You see, Doctor, I regard my suffering as a punishment. I believe in God.

(In itself, logotherapy is a secular approach to clinical problems. However, when a patient stands on the firm ground of religious belief, there can be no objection to making use of the therapeutic effect of his religious convictions and thereby drawing upon his spiritual resources. To this end, the logo-therapist may try to put himself in the place of the patient. That is exactly what I now did.)

F: But cannot suffering sometimes also be a challenge? Is it not conceivable that God wanted to see how Anastasia Kotek will bear it? And perhaps he had to admit, "Yes, she did so very bravely." And now tell me: can anyone remove such an achievement and accomplishment from the world, Frau Kotek?

P: Certainly no one can do it!

F: This remains, doesn't it?

P: It does!

F: By the way, you had no children, had you?

P: I had none.

F: Well, do you think that life is meaningful only when one has children?

P: If they are good children, why shouldn't it be a blessing?

F: Right; but you should not forget that, for instance, the greatest philosopher of all times, Immanuel Kant, had no children; but would anyone venture to doubt the extraordinary meaningfulness of his life? If children were the only meaning of life—life would become meaningless because to procreate something which in itself is meaningless would certainly be the most meaningless thing. What matters in life is rather to achieve something. And this is precisely what you have done. You have made the best of your suffering. You have become an example for our patients because of the way you take your suffering upon yourself. I congratulate you for this achievement, and I also congratulate the other patients who have the opportunity to witness such an example. (*Addressing myself now to my students*): *Ecce homo! (The audience now bursts into spontaneous applause.)* This applause concerns you, Frau Kotek. (*She is weeping now.*) It concerns your life which has been a great achievement. You may be proud of it, Frau Kotek. And how few people may be proud of their lives . . . I should say, your life is a monument. And no one can remove it from the world.

P   (*regaining her self-control*): What you have said, Professor Frankl, is a consolation. It comforts me. Indeed, I never had an opportunity to hear anything like this . . . (*Slowly and quietly she leaves the lecture hall.*)

Apparently, she was reassured. A week later, she died—like Job, one could say—"in a full age." During the last week of her life, however, she was no longer depressed, but on the contrary, full of faith and pride! Prior to this, she had admitted to Dr. Gerda Becker, who was in charge of her on the ward, that she felt agonized, and more specifically, ridden by the anxiety that she was useless. Our interview, however, had made her aware that her life was meaningful and that even her suffering was not in vain. Her last words, immediately before her death, were: "My life is a monument. So Professor Frankl said, to the whole audience, to all the students in the lecture hall. My life was not in vain . . ."

Thus reads the report of Dr. Becker. And we may be justified in assuming that, also like Job, Frau Kotek "came to her grave like as a shock of corn cometh in in his season."

I have said that in this case I drew upon the spiritual resources of my patient. In other words, I left the psychological dimension to enter the noological dimension, the dimension of man's concern with, and search for, ultimate meaning. This was the only proper way to handle the case. I wonder what the outcome would have been if we had invited a behavior therapist to have the patient replace conditioning processes by reconditioning ones . . . And I wonder what the outcome would have been if an orthodox Freudian had confined the interpretation of the case to underlying dynamics. This would have amounted to dodging the actual issue and reinforcing the patient's escapism.

The fact is that a training analysis in the conventional sense does not equip the analyst with what he needs to help such patients as Frau Kotek. "Those who should be able to assist the ill individual," says Professor Travelbee,[7] "either cannot or do not know how to do so. And what can be more demoralizing to an ill individual than to believe that his illness and suffering are meaningless? The tragedy is not that health workers are not always wise enough to help. The tragedy is that the problems are not even recognized by those whose responsibility is to help and comfort."

Another patient of mine whom I interviewed in one of my lectures expressed her concern with the transitoriness of life. "Sooner or later it will be over," she said, "and nothing will be left." I tried to bring her to recognize that the transitoriness of life does not detract from its meaningfulness. I was not successful so I tried a Socratic dialogue. "Have you ever met a man," I asked her, "for whose achievement and accomplishment you have a great respect?" "Certainly," she answered, "our family doctor was a unique person. How he cared for his patients, how he lived for them . . ." "He died?" I inquired. "Yes," she answered. "But his life was exceedingly meaningful, wasn't it," I asked. "If anyone's life is meaningful his life was," she said. "But wasn't this meaningfulness done away with at the moment at which his life was finished?" I asked her. "In no way," she answered, "nothing can alter the fact that his life

[7] Joyce Travelbee, *Interpersonal Aspects of Nursing*, F. A. Davis Company, Philadelphia, 1966, p. 170.

was meaningful." But I continued challenging her: "And what if not a single patient ever remembers what he owes to your family doctor, due to lack of gratitude?" "It remains," she murmured. "Or due to lack of memory?" "It remains." "Or due to the fact that one day the last patient will have died?" "It remains . . ."

That aspect of logotherapy which I call medical ministry must not be confounded with pastoral ministry. The essential difference between the two will be elaborated in the next chapter. For the time being let us ask ourselves whether or not medical ministry is medical at all. Does it in truth belong to the responsibilities of the medical profession to comfort the patient? Emperor Joseph II dedicated the large General Hospital in Vienna, which even today houses most of the university clinics: "*Saluti* et solatio *aegrorum*—to the Care *and Consolation* of the Sick."

I, for one, believe that the words, "Comfort ye, comfort ye my people" (Isaiah 40: 1) are as valid as when they were written and are also addressed to the doctors among "his people."[8] This is the way every good doctor has understood his responsibilities all along. On an unconscious level even the psychoanalyst offers consolation. Consider the cases in which, as Arthur Burton[9] has pointed out, fear of death is indiscriminately analyzed away or reduced to castration anxiety.

In the final analysis this amounts to mistaking a noogenic depression for a psychogenic one. It is similarly commonplace to mistake a somatogenic depression for a psychogenic one. In such a case, the patient is not offered consolation; his self-accusations and guilt feelings are exacerbated, since he feels that he is responsible for the misery in which he finds himself.

[8] "My people" is the vocative rather than the objective. "His people" are not the object but rather the subject of consolation.

[9] Arthur Burton, "Death as a Countertransference," *Psychoanalysis and the Psychoanalytic Review* 49: 3, 1962-1963.

In other words, a psychogenic depression is added to the somatogenic one.

Conversely, marked relief can be brought about by informing the patient of the somatogenic origin of his misery. Pertinent case material has been elaborated on by Schulte, the head of the Department of Psychiatry at the University of Tübingen, in one of his recent publications.

The technique of dereflection helps the patient stop fighting a neurosis or psychosis, spares him the reinforcement of the neurosis or psychosis, and spares him additional suffering. How this is accomplished may be shown in the following excerpts from a tape-recorded interview with a nineteen-year-old schizophrenic girl who was a student at the Vienna Academy of Arts.[10] She had been admitted to my department at the Poliklinik Hospital because she had displayed severe symptoms of incipient schizophrenia, such as auditory hallucinations. She also exhibited the corrugator phenomenon, which I described in 1935.[11] It is characterized by fibrillar twitches of the corrugator muscles and is a typical sign of imminent schizophrenia.

At the outset the patient complains of apathy, then she refers to her "being confused" and asks me for help. So I start dereflecting her:

Frankl: You are in a crisis. You should not concern yourself with any specific diagnosis; let me just say that it is a crisis. Strange thoughts and feelings beset you, I know; but we have made an attempt to tranquilize the rough sea of emo-

[10] Viktor E. Frankl, "Fragments from the Logotherapeutic Treatment of Four Cases," in *Modern Psychotherapeutic Practice: Innovations in Technique,* edited by Arthur Burton, Science and Behavior Books, Palo Alto, California, 1965, pp. 368 ff.
[11] Viktor E. Frankl, "Ein häufiges Phänomen bei Schizophrenie," *Zeitschrift für die gesamte Neurologie und Psychiatrie* 152: 161, 1935.

tion. Through the quieting effects of modern drug treatment we have tried to have you slowly regain your emotional balance. Now you are in a stage where reconstruction of your life is the task awaiting you! But one cannot reconstruct one's life without a life goal, without anything challenging him.

Patient: I understand what you mean, Doctor; but what intrigues me is the question: What is going on within me?

F: Don't brood over yourself. Don't inquire into the source of your trouble. Leave this to us doctors. We will pilot you through the crisis. Well, isn't there a goal beckoning you—say, an artistic accomplishment? Are there not many things fermenting in you—unformed artistic works, undrawn drawings which wait for their creation, as it were, waiting to be produced by you? Think about these things.

P: But this inner turmoil . . .

F: Don't watch your inner turmoil, but turn your gaze to what is waiting for you. What counts is not what lurks in the depths, but what waits in the future, waits to be actualized by you. I know, there is some nervous crisis which troubles you; but let us pour oil on the troubled waters. That is our job as doctors. Leave the problem to the psychiatrists. Anyway, don't watch yourself; don't ask what is going on within yourself, but rather ask what is waiting to be achieved by you. So let's not discuss what we have to deal with in your case: an anxiety neurosis or neurotic obsessions; whatever it may be, let's think of the fact that you are Anna, for whom something is in store. Don't think of yourself, but give yourself to that unborn work which you have to create. And only after you have created it will you come to know what you are like. Anna will be identified as the artist who has accomplished this work. Identity doesn't result from concentration on one's self, but rather from dedication to some cause, from finding one's self through the fulfillment of one's specific work. If I am not mistaken, it was Hölderlin who once wrote: "What we are is nothing; what matters is where we are going." We could say as well: Meaning is more than being.

P: But what is the origin of my trouble?

F: Don't focus on questions like this. Whatever the pathological process underlying your psychological affliction may be, we will cure you. Therefore, don't be concerned with the strange feelings haunting you. Ignore them until we make you get rid of them. Don't watch them. Don't fight them.

(Rather than reinforcing the patient's schizophrenic tendency to autism through plunging into psychodynamic interpretations I try to elicit her will to meaning.)

F: Imagine there are about a dozen great things, works which wait to be created by Anna, and there is no one who could achieve and accomplish it but Anna. No one can replace her in this endeavor. They will be your creations, and if you don't create them, they will remain uncreated forever. If you create them, however, even the devil will be powerless to annihilate them. Then you have rescued them by bringing them to reality. And even if your works were smashed to pieces, in the museum of the past, as I should like to call it, they will remain forever. From this museum, nothing can be stolen since nothing we have done in the past can be undone.

P: Doctor, I believe in what you say. It is a message which makes me happy. (*And with a bright expression on her face, she gets up from the couch and leaves my office.*)

Within a few weeks during which psycho- and pharmaco-therapy were continued, the patient was free from schizophrenic symptomatology to the extent that she could resume her work and study.

Another schizophrenic patient was a seventeen-year-old Jewish youth.[12] His foster father had applied for a single consultation. The young man had been rescued by him during World War II, when a group of Jewish people were executed by the Nazis. Later however, the patient had to be institutionalized in Israel for two and a half years because of severe schizophrenic symptomatology. Now he discusses his problems with me, among others the problem of his detachment from his Jewish theological background, the world in which he was brought up.

Frankl: When did your doubts develop?

Patient: I started doubting when I was in confinement—during my stay at the hospital in Israel. You see, Doctor, the police had caught me and brought me to an institution. And I blamed God for having made me different from normal people.

F: Is it not conceivable, however, that even this was purposeful, in one sense or another? What about Jonah, the prophet who was swallowed by the whale. Wasn't he also "confined"? And why was he?

P: Because God had arranged it, of course.

F: Well, it was certainly no pleasure for Jonah to find himself caught in the bowels of a whale, but only then was it possible for him to recognize the life task which he had previously rejected. Today, I think it is hardly possible to

[12] Viktor E. Frankl, "Fragments from the Logotherapeutic Treatment of Four Cases," in *Modern Psychotherapeutic Practice: Innovations in Technique*, edited by Arthur Burton, Science and Behavior Books, Palo Alto, California, 1965, pp. 370 ff.

institutionalize people in a whale, is it? Anyway, you didn't have to stay in a whale but rather in an institution. Is it inconceivable that through the two and one-half years of confinement God wanted to confront you, too, with a task? Perhaps your confinement was your assignment for a specific period of your life. And didn't you eventually face it in the proper way?

P (*now becoming more emotionally involved, for the first time*): You see, Doctor, that is why I still believe in God.

F: Say more.

P: Possibly God wanted all of that; possibly He wanted me to recover . . .

F: Not just recover, I would say. To recover is no achievement. What is demanded of you is more than recovery. Your spiritual level should be higher than before your illness. Haven't you been in the bowels of a whale for two and one-half years, a little Jonah, as it were? Now you have been freed from what you had to undergo there. Jonah, before his confinement, declined to go to Nineveh to proclaim God; afterward he did so. As to you, it may well be that from now on you will penetrate deeper into the wisdom of the Talmud. I don't wish to say that you should study more than you hitherto did, but your study will be more fruitful and meaningful. For now you have been purified, the way gold and silver, as it is said in the Psalms (or somewhere else), is purified in the furnace.

P: Oh, Doctor, I understand what you mean.

F: Didn't you sometimes weep during your stay in the hospital?

P: Oh, how much I did!

F: Well, through the tears which you wept out of yourself, the clinkers might have been removed from yourself . . .

The impact of the single interview resulted in a remarkable decrease of the patient's aggressiveness toward his foster father and an increase of his interest in the study of the Talmud. For a period of time the patient got a prescription for phenothiazines; later on, he no longer needed further treatment except for small doses of them. He became quite sociable and could resume his handicraft work. Apart from a diminution of initiative, his behavior and conduct are normal. During the single interview outlined above, I succeeded in having the patient reevaluate his plight in the light of meaning and purpose accessible to him, not only despite but because of psychosis. And who would doubt that it was legitimate to draw from the definitely religious resources available in the case? Anyway, I deliberately refrained from analyzing the walls, as it were, which separated the patient from the world. For that matter, I did not care about their origin, be it somatic or psychic. But I did try to challenge the patient out of these walls. In other words, I tried to give him a ground to stand upon.

Sometimes the patient is not only spared additional suffering but also finds additional meaning in suffering. He may even succeed in making suffering into a triumph. Again, however, meaning rests on the attitude the patient chooses toward suffering. The following case might illustrate the point:

A Carmelite sister was suffering from a depression which proved to be somatogenic. She was admitted to the Department of Neurology at the Poliklinik Hospital. Before a specific drug treatment decreased her depression this depression was increased by a psychic trauma. A Catholic priest told her that if she were a true Carmelite sister she would have overcome the depression long before. Of course this was nonsense and it added a psychogenic depression (or, more specifically, an "ecclesiogenic neurosis" as Schaetzing calls it) to her somatogenic depression. But I was able to free the patient of the effects of the traumatic experience and thus relieve her depression over being depressed. The priest had told her that a Carmelite sister cannot be depressed. I told her that perhaps a Carmelite sister alone can master a depression in such an admirable way as she did. In fact, I shall never forget those lines in her diary in which she described the stand she took toward the depression:

"The depression is my steady companion. It weighs my soul down. Where are my ideals, where is the greatness, beauty, and goodness to which I once committed myself? There is nothing but boredom and I am caught in it. I am living as if I were thrown into a vacuum. For there are times at which even the experience of pain is inaccessible to me. And even God is silent. I then wish to die. As soon as possible. And if I did not possess the belief that I am not the master over my life, I would have taken it. By my belief, however, suffering is turned into a gift. People who think that life must be successful are like a man who in the face of a construction site cannot understand that the workers dig out the ground if they wish to build up a cathedral. God builds up a cathedral in each soul. In my soul he is about to dig out the basis. What I have to do is just to keep still whenever I am hit by His shovel."

I think this is more than a case report. It is a *document humain.*

In any event, one is not justified in assuming that a neurosis or psychosis must be detrimental to the religious life of the patient. It need not be a handicap but may well be a challenge and stimulus which triggers a religious response. Even if it is a neurosis that drives a person to religion, religion may become genuine, in the long run, and finally help the person to overcome the neurosis. It therefore is not justified *a priori* to exclude people with neurotic traits from the theological profession. The Biblical promise that truth will make us free does not imply that a truly religious person is in a position to free himself from a neurosis. But neither is the reverse true. That is to say, freedom from neurosis is by no means a guarantee of a religious life. This freedom is neither a necessary nor a sufficient condition for religion.

Only recently I had an opportunity to discuss this issue with a prior who runs a monastery of Benedictine monks and has become quite famous because he accepts anyone as a postulant on two conditions: first, that he will search for God and, second, that he will undergo psychoanalysis. During our conversation he told me that insofar as the writings of Freud, Adler, and Jung are concerned, he had not read a line. He had just undergone psychoanalysis himself, for five years. I doubt that it is justified to insist orthodoxically and dogmatically on the indoctrination along the lines of a particular approach to psychiatry if this insistence is based on personal experience rather than medical practice. The former may be a supplement for the latter but it cannot be a substitute. What is even more important, the lack of psychiatric training, that is to say, the lack of an opportunity to compare one school with another, accounts for much of the proselytizing among psychiatric sectarians.

In an interview with an American magazine, the prior said: "Between 1962, the start of the psychoanalytic era, and 1965, forty-five candidates were entered. Eleven stayed, or a little better than 20 percent."[13] In the face of this figure I must ask myself how few people—if any people at all—would have become and remained psychiatrists if they, too, had been

[13] Robert Serron, "Monks in Analysis," *This Week,* July 3, 1966, pp. 4-14.

screened for neurotic flaws. I, for one, am convinced that unless we have met at least a bit of neuroticism in ourselves, we would not have become psychiatrists because we would not have had an interest in our science, to begin with. And we would not have remained psychiatrists because we would not have had the empathy we need to be good psychiatrists.

A recent study shows that "doctors of medicine are more prone to suicide than are men in other occupations," and what is even more important, "psychiatrists appear to be at the top of the list."[14] Commenting on the high incidence of suicide among physicians, a leading article in a British journal states:[15] "Among the specialties, psychiatry appears to yield a disproportionate number of suicides. The explanation may lie in the choosing of the specialty rather than in meeting its demands, for some who take up psychiatry probably do so for morbid reasons." One might assume that this speaks in favor of personal psychoanalysis to prevent such trainees from becoming psychiatrists, or at least, to assist them in overcoming their morbidity. But alas, on the contrary, "the ominous incidence of suicide among psychiatrists may be blamed on the prevalent notion that undergoing personal psychoanalysis is an essential requirement."[16] Or again to quote Walter Freeman, "the current emphasis upon personal psychoanalysis as a necessity for advancement in the career of the young psychiatrist has dangers that have not been adequately recognized. It is suggested that the insistence upon thorough insight into one's own personality cannot be endured by all who would essay it."

[14] Walter Freeman, "Psychiatrists Who Kill Themselves: A Study in Suicide," *American Journal of Psychiatry* 124: 154, 1967. This is an abridged version of a paper read at the 123rd annual meeting of the American Psychiatric Association, Detroit, Michigan, May 8-12, 1967.

[15] "Suicide Among Doctors," *British Medical Journal* 1: 789, 1964.

[16] Ruth Norden Lowe, "Suicide by Psychiatrists," *American Journal of Psychotherapy* 21: 839, 1967.

I have no *a priori* objection to raise to psychometric approaches in the field of religion in particular and vocation in general. For example, a research project has been launched by James C. Crumbaugh, the research director of the Psychology Service at the Veterans Administration Hospital in Gulfport, Mississippi, and Sister Mary Raphael, O.P., the dean of student affairs at St. Mary's Dominican College in New Orleans, Louisiana. The project is based on the assumption that the will to meaning would be extremely high among the factors which influence members of a religious order. Therefore a sample of sisters of the Dominican Order who are calculated by the nature of their calling to be among those most likely to manifest the will to meaning will be studied by a method of contrasting groups. Psychometric indices of personality, value structure, and purposiveness as measured by the Purpose-in-Life test[17] will be employed to compare a superior versus an inadequate group of nuns in training. The prediction is that the superior group will show strong evidence of behavior which can be most readily interpreted as expressing the will to meaning, while the inadequate group will show a significant lack of such evidence. It is anticipated that the measures of the will to meaning will separate the groups more sharply than the personality measures, and that inclusion of the entire parameter of nun trainees will yield a higher correlation between measures of the will to meaning and measures of trainee proficiency than the correlation between personality measures and trainee proficiency. Dr. Crumbaugh and Sister Mary Raphael are convinced that this motive to find meaning in life exists and is at least to a considerable extent independent of

[17] James C. Crumbaugh and Leonard T. Maholick, " An Experimental Study in Existentialism: The Psychometric Approach to Frankl's Concept of Noogenic Neurosis," *Journal of Clinical Psychology* 20: 200, 1964.

personality variables. If their research project is borne out, they believe that it will then be possible to utilize measures of the will to meaning in various selection procedures as well as in psychodiagnostic testing.

True, this logotherapeutically oriented approach also is psychometrically oriented, i.e., a quantitative approach. In other words, it takes into account various determinants. In a way, it is based on a deterministic concept of man. But a deterministic concept of man is not yet pan-deterministic.

In the context of a pan-deterministic concept of man, it has been hypothesized that by and large the religious life of a person is determined by his father image. However, disbelief cannot always be traced back to a distortion of the father image. I have elaborated on pertinent statistical data collected by my staff in one of my books.[18] Our evidence suggests that religion is not only a matter of education but also decision.

The technique we employed was simple. I had my collaborators screen the patients who visited my out-patient clinic in a single day. This screening showed that twenty-three patients had a positive father image, thirteen a negative one. But only sixteen of the subjects with a positive father image and only two of the subjects with a negative father image had allowed themselves to be fully determined by these images in their religious developments. Half of the total number screened developed their religious concepts independently of their father images. We know that the son of a drunkard does not have to become a drunkard. Similarly a poor religious life cannot always be traced back to the impact of a negative father image. Nor does even the worst father image necessarily prevent one from establishing a sound relation to God (see

[18] Viktor E. Frankl, *Psychotherapy and Existentialism: Selected Papers on Logotherapy*, Washington Square Press, New York, 1967.

the eleven subjects). Thus half of the subjects displayed what education had made of them, and the other half showed what, by way of decision, they had made of themselves.[19]

Facts are not fate. What matters is the stand we take toward them. People need not become bad monks and nuns because of a neurosis, but may well become good monks and nuns in spite of it. In some cases, they even become good monks and nuns because of a neurosis. And what holds for monks and nuns also is true of psychiatrists. In fact, such creative psychiatrists as the founders of the pioneering schools are said to have developed systems which in the final analysis depict their own neuroses. In this I would see an achievement, for in this way they have not only overcome their own neuroses but also taught other doctors how to help their patients overcome their neuroses. The misery of a single man is turned into a sacrifice for the sake of mankind. The only question is whether the neurosis of a given psychiatrist is representative of the neuroses of the time in which he lives. If it is, his suffering stands for the suffering of humanity. One must go through his own existential despair if he is to learn how to immunize his patients against it.

Let me return to my contention that a neurotic is religious or irreligious irrespective of being a neurotic. Neurosis is not necessarily detrimental to religion. The neurotic may be re-

[19] Here I am prepared to meet an objection from theologians, since one might say that building up one's religious belief in spite of unfavorable educational conditions is inconceivable without the intervention of divine grace. If man is to believe in God, he has to be helped by grace. But one should not forget that my investigation moves within the frame of reference of psychology, or rather anthropology: that is to say, on the human level. Grace, however, dwells in the supra-human dimension and therefore appears on the human plane only as a projection. In other words, what on the natural plane takes on the appearance of being man's decision might well be interpreted on the supra-natural plane as the sustaining assistance of God.

ligious either despite or because of being neurotic. This fact reflects the independence and authenticity of religion. To all appearances religion is indestructible and indelible. Even psychosis cannot destroy it.

A man of about sixty was brought to me because of auditory hallucinations lasting over many decades. I was facing a ruined personality. Everyone in his environment regarded him as an idiot. Yet what a strange charm radiated from this man! As a child he had wanted to become a priest. However, he had had to be content with the only joy he could experience, and that was singing in the church choir on Sunday mornings. Now, his sister, who accompanied him, reported that although he was very excitable, he was always ultimately able to regain his self-control. I became interested in the psychodynamics underlying the case, for I thought the patient had a strong fixation on his sister; so I asked him how he managed to regain his self-control: "For whose sake do you do so?" Thereupon, there was a pause of some seconds, and then the patient answered: "For God's sake."

"For God's sake," he said. In other words, *to please God.* In this context I would like to quote Kierkegaard, who once said: "Even if insanity holds up the fool's garment to me, I can save my soul if I want *to please God.*" That is to say, even if I am afflicted with psychosis I can choose my attitude to my predicament and by so doing transmute it into an achievement.

For a change let me speak of a case of manic-depressive psychosis rather than schizophrenia. I shall never forget one of the most beautiful girls I have ever met. She was Jewish, but she stayed in Vienna for some time even under Hitler because her father was an official employed by the Jewish community. During a manic period she went through, her father consulted me because of her promiscuity. I pointed out that there are two main dangers involved in manic periods, namely, contracting venereal diseases and becoming pregnant. In this case, there was a third danger: life danger. She visited nightclubs in the company of SS men. She danced with them and went to bed with them, endangering them as well as herself. Finally, she was sent to a concentration camp. There I saw her again. And I shall never forget the scene. I cannot but compare it with the last scene of the last act of the first part of Goethe's *Faust*. Like Gretchen she was kneeling on straw in an underground vault in the midst of a crowd of psychotic people who wallowed in feces. She was folding her hands, looking upward and murmuring prayers. "*Shema Yisrael* . . ." When she saw me, she clung to me and implored me to forgive her. I tried to quiet her. When I left her she continued murmuring prayers. In Hebrew. Except for this circumstance, like Gretchen. About an hour later she died. She had been bodily exhausted, mentally disturbed, and severely disoriented. She didn't know where she was, or why. She only knew how to pray.

In the face of a case such as the schizophrenic old man and the manic-depressive girl, one is tempted to reinterpret a verse in the Psalms which reads: "The Lord is nigh unto them that are of a broken heart; and saveth such as be of a contrite spirit." Is it not a characteristic of the developmental curve of schizophrenic patients that it is "broken"? Is it not a characteristic of manic-depressive patients that they are "contrite"? And are not schizophrenic and manic-depressive patients sometimes closer to religion than the average?

Even a retarded child retains the humanness of human beings. And Carl J. Rote, resident chaplain in a state institution of some 4,300 mentally retarded patients, deserves a hearing:

"The retardates have taught me more than I can ever tell. Theirs is a world where hypocrisy is banished; it is a kingdom where a smile is their passport to your affection and the light in their eyes will melt the coldest heart. Perhaps this is God's way of reminding us that the world must rediscover the attributes which the mentally retarded have never lost!"[20]

One cannot but subscribe to a statement made by W. M. Millar, Professor of Mental Health at Aberdeen University in Scotland: "There is surely something wrong in the idea that wholeness must be equated with mental health, that an individual in the eyes of God is not complete unless he has a certificate of fitness from a psychiatrist. What about the idiot child, or the withdrawn schizophrenic, or the demented senile patient? What comfort can be brought to them if we commit ourselves to this notion of physical-mental integrity? There must surely be some sense in which these creatures of God can be made whole, although there can be no hope of their medical recovery."[21]

In the light of logotherapy this does not imply taking sides in the issue between theism and humanism. For in the light of logotherapy religion is a human phenomenon, and as a human phenomenon it must be taken earnestly. It must be taken at face value and not dismissed by being reduced to subhuman phenomena along the lines of reductionism.

Taking religion seriously allows for drawing upon the spiritual resources of the patient. In this context spiritual means uniquely and truly human. And in this sense medical ministry is a legitimate task of the doctor.

[20] Carl J. Rote, "Mental Retardation: The Cry of Why?" *Association of Mental Hospital Chaplains Newsletter* 2: 41, 1965.
[21] W. M. Millar, "Mental Health and Spiritual Wholeness," *Journal of Societal Issues* 1: 7, 1964.

Certainly we can manage without it and still be doctors but
—to allude to a bon mot made by Paul Dubois—we should
realize that then the only thing which makes us different from
the veterinarians is the clientele.

CONCLUSION

DIMENSIONS OF MEANING

❦ ❦ ❦ ALLOWANCE must be made for the fact that not everything I am going to present in the framework of this chapter is a tenet of logotherapy. By the very nature of the subject matter I cannot but include the confession of many personal convictions on the borderline between theology and psychiatry.

There are too many psychiatrists dabbling in the field of theology and too many theologians dabbling in the field of psychiatry. E. Frederick Proells, resident chaplain of the penitentiary of the City of New York, refers to "half-baked minister-psychologists who jettison their religious weapons." They "would be put to shame," he continues, "by some medical doctors who were doing remarkable work by just using religious means, having gone back and picked up what the mixed-up theologians had left out."[1] I would say, however, that the psychiatrists should resist the temptation in turn to dabble in the field of theology. Time and again I am asked the question, "Where is a place for grace in logotherapy?" And I answer that a doctor writing up a prescription or per-

[1] E. Frederick Proells, "Reflections of the Social, Moral, Cultural, and Spiritual Aspects of the Prison Chaplain's Ministry," *Journal of Pastoral Care* 12: 69, 1958.

forming an operation should do so as attentively as possible, but he should not flirt with grace. The more he pays attention to what he is doing, and the less he cares for grace, the better a vehicle he will be for grace. The more human one is, the more he can be a tool for divine purposes.

Logotherapy does not cross the boundary between psychotherapy and religion. But it leaves the door to religion open and it leaves it to the patient whether or not to pass the door. It is the patient who has to decide whether he interprets responsibleness in terms of being responsible to humanity, society, conscience, or God. It is up to him to decide to what, to whom, and for what he is responsible.

Many writers in the field of logotherapy have pointed out that it is compatible with religion. However, logotherapy is not a Protestant, Catholic, or Jewish psychotherapy.[2] A religious psychotherapy in the proper sense is inconceivable because of the essential difference between psychotherapy and religion, which is a dimensional difference. To begin with, the aims of the two are different. Psychotherapy aims at mental health. Religion aims at salvation. It is true, as Howard Chandler Robbins wrote, that "worship tranquilizes the mind. But it cannot be practiced for this purpose without the self-defeat of the purpose. We do not sing our Te Deum, our Gloria in Excelsis, in the hope of curing insomnia or getting rid of chronic indigestion. We sing our Te Deum, our Gloria in Excelsis, to the glory of God."

Moreover, logotherapy must be available for every patient and usable in the hands of every doctor, whether his *Weltanschauung* is theistic or agnostic. This availability is essential on the basis of the Hippocratic oath, if for no other reason.

[2] The late Leo Baeck's conviction that logotherapy is "the" Jewish psychotherapy is understandable in view of the fact that he once translated "torah" as "life task."

On the other hand, while a psychotherapist is not and must not be concerned with the religious life of his patient, he may well contribute to it as an unintended side effect. Pertinent case material is included in the volume, *Psychotherapy and Existentialism*.[3]

An analogous by-product is religion's inestimable contribution to mental health. After all, religion provides man with a spiritual anchor, with a feeling of security such as he can find nowhere else.[4]

Fusion of psychotherapy and religion necessarily results in confusion, for such fusion confounds two different dimensions, the dimensions of anthropology and theology. As compared with the dimension of anthropology, that of theology is the higher one in that it is more inclusive.

How then is it possible, in the face of the dimensional difference between the human world and the divine world, for man to recognize this difference? To understand this difference we need only consider the relation between man and animals. The human world includes the world of the animal. In a way man can understand the animal, but the animal cannot understand man. Now it is my contention that the ratio between man and the animal is somewhat similar to the ratio between God and man.

In one of my books[5] I have elaborated this analogy: an ape that is being used to develop poliomyelitis serum, and for this reason is punctured again and again, is not able to grasp the meaning of its suffering, for with its limited intelligence it

[3] Viktor E. Frankl, *Psychotherapy and Existentialism: Selected Papers on Logotherapy*, Washington Square Press, New York, 1967.

[4] Viktor E. Frankl, *The Doctor and the Soul: From Psychotherapy to Logotherapy*, second, expanded edition, Alfred A. Knopf, New York, 1965 (paperback edition: Bantam Books, New York, 1967).

[5] Viktor E. Frankl, *Man's Search for Meaning: An Introduction to Logotherapy*, Washington Square Press, New York, 1963, p. 187.

cannot enter into the world of man, the only world in which its suffering is understandable. Is it not conceivable that there is still another dimension possible, a world beyond man's world, a world in which the question of an ultimate meaning of human suffering will find an answer?

Now let us take another example, a dog. If I point to something with my finger, the dog does not look in the direction in which I point; it looks at my finger and sometimes snaps at my finger. It cannot understand the semantic function of pointing to something. And what about man? Is not he, too, sometimes unable to understand the meaning of something, say, the meaning of suffering, and does not he, too, quarrel with his fate and snap at its finger?

Man is incapable of understanding the ultimate meaning of human suffering because "mere thinking cannot reveal to us the highest purpose," as Albert Einstein once said. I would say that the ultimate meaning, or as I prefer to call it, the supra-meaning is no longer a matter of thinking but rather a matter of believing. We do not catch hold of it on intellectual grounds but on existential grounds, out of our whole being, i.e., through faith.

But it is my contention that faith in the ultimate meaning is preceded by trust in an ultimate being, by trust in God. Imagine a dog—another dog—a dog which is ill. You bring it to a veterinarian and he brings pain to the dog. It looks up, looks at you, and now lets the veterinarian examine and treat it. In spite of pain the dog keeps quiet. It cannot understand the meaning of pain, the purpose of a shot or a bandage, but the way it looks at you reveals a boundless trust in you, out of which it feels that the doctor will not harm it.

Man cannot break through the dimensional difference between the human world and the divine world but he can reach out for the ultimate meaning through faith which is mediated by trust in the ultimate being. But God is "high above all the blessings and hymns, praises and consolations, which are uttered in the world," as it is said in the famous Hebrew prayer for the dead, Kaddish. That is to say, again we meet a dimensional difference, one comparable with what Martin Heidegger calls the ontological difference, the essential difference between things and being. Heidegger holds that being is not one thing among other things. A few years ago a little boy told my wife that he knew what he was going to be when he grew up. She asked what it would be and he answered, "Either I'll be an acrobat on a trapeze in a circus or I'll be God." He dealt with God as if being God were one vocation among other vocations.

The ontological difference between being and things or for that matter the dimensional difference between the ultimate being and human beings, prevents man from really speaking of God. Speaking of God implies making being into a thing. It implies reification. Personification would be justified. In other words, man cannot speak of God but he may speak to God. He may pray.

The famous sentence by which Ludwig Wittgenstein concludes his most famous book, reads: "Whereof one cannot speak, thereof one must be silent." It has been translated into many languages. Let me translate it from the agnostic into the theistic language. It would then read: "To Him of Whom one cannot speak, to Him one must pray."

However, recognizing the dimensional difference between the human world and the divine world not only detracts from but also adds to knowledge and makes for wisdom. If a problem cannot be solved we may at least understand why it is unsolvable. Consider the saying that God writes straight on crooked lines. This is inconceivable on the plane of a page on which we imagine that God is writing. Writing straight means

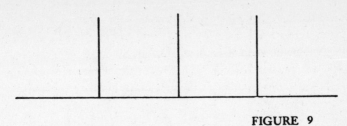

FIGURE 9

writing straight on straight lines

FIGURE 10

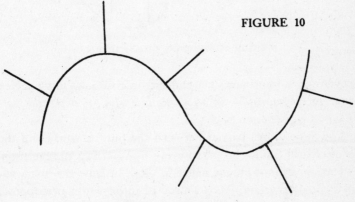

writing on crooked lines

setting parallel letters perpendicular to the lines. On crooked lines the letters cannot be parallel. But if we consider a three-dimensional space rather than the two-dimensional plane of the page, it is perfectly possible to set parallel letters on crooked lines. In other words, on the grounds of the dimensional difference between the human world and the divine world we may take a step beyond the step taken by Socrates, who said that he only knew that he did not know anything. We now know the reason why we cannot know everything. We understand why we cannot understand everything. What

FIGURE 11

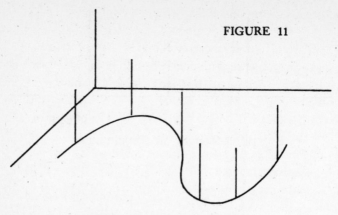

writing straight on crooked lines

is even more important, we understand that *something which seems to be impossible in a lower dimension, is perfectly possible in a higher one.*

The dimensional barrier between the human world and the divine world cannot be talked away by referring to revelation. Revelation cannot induce belief in God, because the acknowledgment of revelation as a source of information presupposes belief in God. An unbeliever never acknowledges that revelation is a historical fact.

Argumentation on logical grounds is not more valid than the argumentation on historical grounds. From petrified footprints you may infer that dinosaurs have existed. But from natural things you cannot infer that a supra-natural being exists. God is no petrifaction. Teleology is not a reliable bridge between anthropology and theology.

To the unbeliever both the historical way and the logical way of argumentation are but two stumbling blocks. But there is also a third one, anthropomorphism. I would define anthropomorphism as theology in terms of anthropology. Or, to put it in a lighter vein, God as the grandfather image. An instance that illustrates the point is the following joke:

A Sunday school teacher once told her class a story of a poor man whose wife had died in childbirth. He could not afford to hire a wet nurse, but God worked a miracle by letting breasts grow on the chest of the poor man so that the newborn baby could be suckled. One of the boys, however, objected that there was no need to work a miracle. Why did not God simply arrange for the poor man to find an envelope with a thousand dollars to pay a wet nurse? But the teacher replied: "You are a silly boy. If God can work a miracle he certainly will not throw away cash." Why do we laugh? Because a certain human category, namely, saving cash, has been applied to the motivations of God.

The three stumbling blocks, authoritarianism, rationalism, and anthropomorphism, account for much of the repression in the field of religion. I am in a position to quote a case in which repressed religious feelings were revealed by X rays. I owe the report to H. E. Blumenthal of the Hebrew University in Jerusalem. "[It] concerns a woman of middle age who was admitted to hospital because of severe colitis. She emphasized to the doctor in the X-ray department that she was not a religious person, but that she got the attack especially after having eaten pork. The first screening after a barium meal showed the colon quite normal. On the second occasion she was given the barium meal and was told that it contained pork; the result was severe attacks of colitis after the X ray. For the third picture pork was in fact mixed with the barium meal, but without the patient being told about it. This time the X ray again showed a perfectly normal colon, and the woman had no attack afterwards."[6]

[6] H. E. Blumenthal, "Jewish Challenge to Freud," *Here and Now*, 1: 24, 1955, p. 12.

In a book of mine which has not yet been translated into English,[7] I have included unconsciously religious dreams of consciously atheistic patients. And I have watched agnostic patients lying on their deathbeds, knowing that they were going to die, and yet having in them a sense of shelteredness which cannot be explained by their irreligious philosophy of life.[8] But it may well be explained by the assumption of what I would call the basic trust in an ultimate meaning. Albert Einstein gave the definition that to find a satisfying answer to the question, "What is the meaning of life?" means to be religious. If we subscribe to his definition of religion we are justified in claiming that man is basically religious.

In the strict sense of Immanuel Kant's transcendentalism,[9] man's trust in meaning would deserve to be called transcendental. If I am allowed for didactic reasons to oversimplify matters, man really cannot perceive things without perceiving them in space and time and applying to them the category of cause and effect. So far Kant. Now it is my contention that man really could not move a limb unless deep down to the foundations of existence, and out of the depths of being, he is imbued by a basic trust in the ultimate meaning. Without

[7] Viktor E. Frankl, *Der unbewusste Gott,* Amandus-Verlag, Wien, 1948.

[8] Usually death is compared with sleep. Actually, however, dying should be compared with being wakened. At least this comparison makes it comprehensible that death is beyond comprehension. Consider a loving father tenderly waking his child with a caressing touch. The child will wake up with a start, with fright, because in his dream world into which the touch intrudes, its proper meaning cannot be conceived. Man, too, wakes up, from life to death, with fright. And if, after being clinically dead, his life is saved it is understandable that he does not remember anything. The waker remembers his dreams, but the dreamer does not know that he is sleeping.

[9] In my opinion Kant by his trancendentalism has turned a *quaestio iuris* into a *quaestio facti* in that the question whether or not we are justified in using certain categories, is answered by showing that we cannot do without them, and that we have been using them all along. There is no point in questioning what we must do.

it he would have to stop breathing. Even a person who commits suicide must be convinced that suicide makes sense.

Thus trust in meaning and faith in being, however dormant they may be, are transcendental and hence indispensable. They cannot be done away with. We have discussed cases in which they have been repressed because a person felt ashamed of religious feelings. Such a person had been confronted with an image of religion without justice being done to the dimensional difference between the human world and the divine world. But there are also people who are not too much aware of this difference, but too little aware of it. I mean those people who insist that nothing can be real unless it is tangible. They are not even aware of the dimensional difference between somatic and psychic phenomena. But these people may be reached by reference to what they have been presupposing all along. Let me illustrate the idea:

In the setting of a discussion a young man asked whether it was justified to speak of a soul if it cannot be seen. Even if we explore the brain tissue in a microscope, he said, we will never find anything such as a soul. Now the moderator asked me to handle the issue. And I started by asking the young man what motivated him in raising the question. "My intellectual honesty," he answered. "Well," I continued challenging him, "is it bodily? Is it tangible? Will it be visible in a microscope?" "Of course, it won't," he admitted, "because it is mental." "Aha," I said, "in other words, what you were searching for in vain in the microscope is a condition for your search, and presupposed by you all along, isn't it?"

When Martin Heidegger visited Vienna the first time in his life, he offered a privatissimum seminar to a dozen scholars. In the evening of the same day Professor G. of the Department of Philosophy at the University of Vienna and I took Heidegger out to a Viennese Heuriger (a typical Viennese place where the owner of a vineyard sells his own wine). Our wives were with us. Since the wife of Professor G. was not a professional philosopher but rather a former opera star, she asked me to explain in plain words what the outcome had been in the seminar with Heidegger. I improvised the following story: "Once upon a time there was a man who stood behind a telescope and was despairing because, as he said, he had searched all around the sky for some planet of the solar system, but could not find it. Specifically, it was a planet whose name was Earth. A friend referred him to a sage whose name was Martin Heidegger. 'What are you searching for?' Heidegger asked the astronomer. 'The earth,' the man lamented, 'and nowhere in the whole firmament could I find it.' 'And may I ask you where you have set the tripod?' inquired Heidegger. 'On the earth, of course,' was the immediate reply. 'O.K.,' concluded Heidegger, 'here it is.'"

What one was in search of, again, had been presupposed all along. Literally pre-sup-posed, that is to say, (posed) laid (sup) under (underlying) his search (pre) before even setting out on it.

Martin Heidegger asked my permission to use this image in his lectures. He lets himself be led by etymologies. Why should I not let myself be guided by analogies?

People who limit reality to what is tangible and visible and for this reason tend *a priori* to deny the existence of an ultimate being, also repress religious feelings. Along with those people who are too sophisticated to embrace naive concepts of religion, there are people who are too immature to overcome a primitive epistemology. They insist that God must be visible. But if they had ever stood on a stage they could have learned a lesson. Blinded by the footlights and spotlights a man on stage cannot see the audience. Instead of an audience there is a huge black hole. He cannot see the people who are watching him. And man, standing on the stage of life and playing a role in life, cannot see before whom he is playing the role. He cannot see before whom he is responsible for properly playing the role. In the blinding lights of what happens in the foreground of everyday life, he sometimes forgets that he is watched, that hidden in the dark someone sits in a box and watches him, he who "made darkness his hiding place," as it is said in a Psalm. And we often feel an impulse to remind him that the curtain is up and whatever he does is watched.

In North Korean prisoner of war camps the prisoners were told that if they did not yield to brainwashing, they would die without anybody knowing about them and their heroism. To someone who is not religious, it must seem senseless to be heroic if no one gets anything out of it, and not even a single person ever knows anything about it.[10]

The huge black hole is filled with symbols. Man is the being which is capable of creating symbols, and a being in need of symbols. His languages are systems of symbols. So are his religions. And what holds for the languages is also true of the religions. That is to say, nobody is justified in claiming, out of a superiority complex, that one language is superior to another. For it is possible in each language to arrive at truth—at the one truth—and equally is it possible in each language to err—and to lie.

I do not think the trend is away from religion per se. But I do think that the trend is away from those religions, or rather denominations, whose representatives are concerned with attacking and fighting each other. This was my answer after the local reporter of *Time* magazine had called me by telephone and asked me the question, Is God dead? As he told me that this question was going to be a cover story, I first

---

[10] Joost A. M. Meerloo, "Pavlovian Strategy as a Weapon of Menticide," *American Journal of Psychiatry* 110: 809, 1954.

asked whether the editor was going in the end to select God "Man of the Year."

After I had pointed out that the trend is not away from religion but only away from emphasis on the differences between the individual denominations, the *Time* reporter asked me whether I meant that the trend away from denominations is in favor of some sort of universal religion. This, however, I definitely denied. Rather the contrary is true. The trend moves toward a profoundly personalized religion, so that every man will arrive at a language of his own, find the words of his own, when addressing himself to the ultimate being.

But what about the issue at hand, Is God dead? I would say that God is not dead but silent. Silent, however, he has been all along. The "living" God has been a "hidden" God all along. You must not expect him to answer your call. If you probe the depth of the sea, you send off sound waves and wait for the echo from the bottom of the sea. If God exists, however, he is infinite, and you wait for an echo in vain. The fact that no answer comes back to you is proof that your call has reached the addressee, the infinite.

If you look at the sky you cannot see the sky because whatever you may see on the sky is not the sky itself but on the contrary hiding the sky, say, a cloud. From the infinite height called the sky—the ways of God are said to be as much above the ways of man as the sky is above the earth—from the infinite height no light is reflected—and from the infinite depth no sound is returned.

Gordon W. Allport, in his renowned book, *The Individual and His Religion*, refers to a profoundly personalized religion when he speaks of the Hindu religion. There are "varying conceptions of deity held by different individuals and by one and the same individual at different periods of time. When we need affection, God is love; knowledge, He is omniscient; consolation, He granteth peace that passeth understanding. When we have sinned, he is the Redeemer; when we need guidance, the Holy Spirit. An interesting rite in the Hindu religion here comes to mind. Around the age of sixteen or eighteen, the Hindu youth receives from his teacher a name for God which all his life long shall serve this youth as a private instrument for prayer and for binding himself to the Deity. In this custom Hinduism recognizes that the temperament, needs, and capacities of the initiate himself must in large part determine his approach to religious verities. In this practice we have a rare instance of an institutional religion recognizing the ultimate individuality of the religious sentiment. In India it is not enough that each individual should have a name for the deity suited to his own personal needs; it is also strictly advised that this name be kept secret even from one's bosom friends and from one's spouse. In the last analysis each person confronts his deity in solitude, and it is thought well to symbolize this fact, especially in overcrowded households and communities, with the seal of secrecy."[11]

Is this to imply that the individual denominations, or for that matter organizations and institutions in the field of religion will disappear? By no means. However different the personal styles may be in which man expresses himself and addresses himself to the ultimate being, there are symbols which are shared, and a common store of symbols always will remain. Are not there languages which despite all differences have the same alphabet in common?

At the conclusion let me remind myself of being an M.D. in the first place. Day by day I am confronted with people

[11] Gordon W. Allport, *The Individual and His Religion*, The Macmillan Company, New York, 1956, pp. 10 ff.

who are incurable, men who become senile, and women who remain sterile. I am besieged by their cry for an answer to the question of an ultimate meaning to suffering.

I myself went through this purgatory when I found myself in a concentration camp and lost the manuscript of the first version of my first book. Later, when my own death seemed imminent, I asked myself what my life had been for. Nothing was left which would survive me. No child of my own. Not even a spiritual child such as the manuscript. But after wrestling with my despair for hours, shivering from typhus fever, I finally asked myself what sort of meaning could depend on whether or not a manuscript of mine is printed. I would not give a damn for it. But if there is meaning, it is unconditional meaning, and neither suffering nor dying can detract from it.

And what our patients need is unconditional faith in unconditional meaning. Remember what I have said of life's transitoriness. In the past nothing is irrecoverably lost but everything is irrevocably stored. People only see the stubble field of transitoriness but overlook the full granaries of the past in which they have delivered and deposited, in which they have saved, their harvest.

But what about those miserable creatures whose granaries are empty, as it were, what about the senile men, the sterile women, and those artists and scientists whose desks and drawers are empty rather than full of manuscripts? What about them? The unconditional faith in an unconditional meaning may turn the complete failure into a heroic triumph. That this is possible has not only been demonstrated by many a patient in our days but also by a peasant who lived in Biblical times, somewhere in Palestine. His were granaries in the literal sense. And they were literally empty. And yet, out of an unconditional trust in ultimate meaning and an unconditional faith in ultimate being, Habakkuk chanted his triumphant hymn:

"Although the fig tree shall not blossom, neither shall fruit be in the vines; the labor of the olive shall fail, and the fields shall yield no meat; the flock shall be cut off from the fold, and there shall be no herd in the stalls: Yet I will rejoice in the Lord, I will joy in the God of my salvation."

May this be the lesson to learn from my book.

AFTERWORD:
THE DE-GURUFICATION OF
LOGOTHERAPY

For the First World Congress of Logotherapy, held in San Diego in 1980, I was asked to give the opening address. The organizers of the event were specific regarding the format of the speech. I was to elaborate—and I quote literally—"how I envisage logotherapy after I am gone." In other words, I was to deliver a swansong, deposit a legacy. But I am not a prophet to foresee the future of logotherapy, even less a guru to decree what its future should be. The title, in fact, that I chose for my address was "Logotherapy on Its Way to De-gurufication," because the future of logotherapy is dependent on all logotherapists.

I am a descendant of the Maharal of Prague, the legendary Rabbi made famous by the novel *The Golem* and from the movies based on this novel. The Rabbi was an intimate friend of the contemporary Emperor of Austria, and the Golem was a robot that the Rabbi had created out of clay. However, a dozen generations separate me from my revered ancestor, and in the meantime, any concern with creating robots has evaporated and dissipated. I have neither an interest in creating robots nor raising parrots that just rehash their master's voice. But I do wish for the future that the cause of logotherapy be taken over and carried out by independent and inventive, innovative and creative spirits. Logotherapy regards man as being in search of meaning and responsible for its fulfillment. Logotherapy sees its own assignment in making man conscious of "being responsible," of his "responsibleness." This also holds for the logotherapist himself inasmuch as he, too, should be aware of his responsibleness. In other words, he should be characterized by an independent spirit.

It goes to the credit of Reuven P. Bulka[1] to have defended logotherapy against the accusation of being "authoritarian." And in a recent book on logotherapy, the author, Elisabeth S. Lukas,[2] states that throughout the history of psychotherapy, there has never been a school as undogmatic and as open as logotherapy. In fact, logotherapy may well be called an open system. However, we do not only confess to its openness but also to its being a system. After all, *"el sistema es el orgullo del pensador,"* as Ortega y Gasset said: "the system is the pride of the thinker." J.B. Torello[3] did not even hesitate to claim that in the history of psychotherapy, logotherapy is the last school whose teaching body has been developed in terms of a systematically organized structure.

This does not do away with, or detract from, my being "The Father of Logotherapy," as the journal *Existential Psychiatry* has called me. And the Latin dictum according to which fatherhood is never certain (*pater semper incertus*) is not applicable as far as logotherapy is concerned. But my being the father, or let us simply say founder, of logotherapy, means no more than having laid its foundation; and a foundation, in turn, means no less than an invitation extended to others to continue constructing the building on the basis of the foundation. Reading and rereading my books spares them reinventing logotherapy and thus saves time for their share in its further development.

Logotherapy is a system open in a twofold sense inasmuch as it is open toward its own evolution as well as toward the cooperation with other schools. That this twofold openness has borne fruit already is evidenced by the fact that so far no less than forty authors (myself not included) have turned out fifty-seven books on logotherapy, published in fifteen languages, not

[1]Reuven P. Bulka, "Is Logotherapy Authoritarian?" *Journal of Humanistic Psychology* 18 (4), 1978, 45–54.

[2]Elisabeth S. Lukas, *Auch dein Leben hat Sinn: Logotherapeutisch Wege zur Gesundung,* Freiburg, Herder, 1980.

[3]J.B. Torello, "Viktor E. Frankl, l'homme," in Viktor E. Frankl, *La psychotherapie et son image de l'homme,* Paris, Resma, 1970.

to mention the 104 dissertations on the same subject. And all the authors are moving on various levels of sophistication— covering the whole spectrum from popularizing, not to say vulgarizing, literature, to empirically oriented, even experimentally based publications—and they are moving in different directions. As the difference of viewpoints sometimes eventuates in results deviating from each other, we may ask: "What then is still, and what is no longer, logotherapy?" I could simply and easily answer this question by stating that logotherapy pure and proper is just what you find in my books. But confessing to the community of logotherapists does not necessitate subscription to whatever Dr. Frankl has said or written.

A reader can only apply what he has found convincing. You cannot persuade others of anything of which you are not convinced yourselves! This particularly applies to the logotherapist's conviction that life does have a meaning and that it is even unconditionally meaningful, up to its last moment, to one's last breath, and that death itself may be endowed with meaning. And in case a reader *does* subscribe to this belief, he can find in my writings all the arguments that he needs to strengthen this belief. If inclined toward the latter position, that life is unconditionally meaningful, we may redefine the helping professions as called upon more specifically to help their patients in the basic and ultimate human aspiration of finding a meaning in their lives. And by so doing, those who belong to the helping professions retroactively find a vocation and mission themselves, for their own lives. When I was asked by the editor of *Who's Who in America* to epitomize my life in a few lines, I did so with the words you may be able to guess: "I have seen the meaning of my life in helping others to see in their lives a meaning."

The evolution of logotherapy not only concerns its applications in various fields but also its foundations. A lot of work has been done, by a host of authors, to consolidate, corroborate, and validate those findings which, for too long a time, had been based on solely intuitive grounds, more specifically, on the intuitions of a teenager named Viktor E. Frankl. Now, logotherapy has become scientifically established on the grounds of research based on (1) tests, (2) statistics, and (3) experiments:

1. So far, we have the ten logotherapeutic tests of Walter Bockmann, James C. Crumbaugh, Bernard Dansart, Bruno Giorgi, Ruth Hablas, R.R. Hutzell, Gerald Kovacic, Elisabeth S. Lukas, Leonard T. Maholick, and Patricia L. Starck.

2. As to statistics, we can point to the outcome of research conducted by Brown, Casciani, Crumbaugh, Dansart, Durlak, Kratochvil, Lukas, Lunceford, Mason, Meier, Murphy, Planova, Popeilski, Richmond, Roberts, Ruch, Sallee, Smith, Yarnell, and Young. Their work constitutes the empirical evidence that, indeed, people can find, and fulfill, a meaning in their lives irrespective of gender or age, IQ or educational background, environment or character structure, and finally irrespective of whether or not one is religious, and if he is, irrespective of the denomination to which he may belong. The authors have computerized hundreds of thousands of data obtained from thousands of subjects in order to find empirical evidence of the unconditional potential meaningfulness of life.

But also with regard to the opposite, the feeling of meaninglessness or, better to say, the noogenic neurosis deriving from it, much has been done by way of statistics. I am referring to the research projects that, although conducted independently of each other, arrived at the consistent conclusion that about twenty percent of neuroses are noogenic of nature and origin: the work of Frank M. Buckley, Eric Klinger, Dietrich Langen, Elisabeth S. Lukas, Eva Niebauer-Kozdera, Kazimierz Popielski, Hans Joachim Prill, Nina Toll, Ruth Volhard, and T.A. Werner.

3. As to experiments, L. Solyom, F. Garza-Perez, B.L. Ledwidge, and C. Solyom[4] were the first to offer experi-

[4]L. Solyom, J. Garza-Perez, B.L. Ledwidge and C. Solyom, "Paradoxical Intention in the Treatment of Obsessive Thoughts: A Pilot Study," *Comprehensive Psychiatry* 13 (3), 1972, 291–297.

mental evidence that the logotherapeutic technique of paradoxical intention is effective. More recently, L. Michael
Ascher and Ralph M. Turner [5,6] have come up with a
controlled experimental validation of the clinical effectiveness of paradoxical intention in comparison with other
behavioral strategies.

As much as we may appreciate the scientific foundation of
logotherapy, we are aware of the toll it takes. I suspect that
logotherapy has become too scientific to become popular in the
proper sense of the word. Ironically, it is too revolutionary to
be fully acceptable in scientific circles. Small wonder. The
concept of a will to meaning as the basic motivation of man is a
slap in the face of all the current motivation theories, which still
are based on the homeostasis principle, regarding man as a
being who is just out to satisfy drives and instincts, to gratify
needs, and all this just in order to maintain or restore an inner
equilibrium, a state without tensions. And all the fellow-beings
he seems to love, and all the causes he seems to serve, are seen
as mere tools serving him to get rid of the tensions aroused by
the drives and the instincts and the needs as soon, and as long,
as they are not satisfied and gratified. In other words, self-
transcendence, which logotherapy considers the essence of human existence, has been totally left out of the picture of man
that underlies the current motivation theories. Yet man is
neither a being who is just abreacting his instincts, nor a being
who is just reacting to stimuli, but he is a being who is acting
into a world, a "being-in-the-world," to avail myself of the
(more-often-than-not misinterpreted) Heideggerian phraseology,
and the world wherein he is, is a world replete with other

[5]Ralph M. Turner and L. Michael Ascher, "Controlled Comparison of
Progressive Relaxation, Stimulus Control, and Paradoxical Intention Therapies
for Insomnia." *Journal of Consulting and Clinical Psychology* 47 (3), 1979,
500–508.

[6]L. Michael Ascher and Ralph M. Turner, "A Comparison of Two Methods
for the Administration of Paradoxical Intention." *Behav. Res. and Therapy*
18, 1980, 121–126.

beings and those meanings toward which he is transcending himself. But how can we come to grips with the ills and ailments of our time, which are grounded in a frustration of the will to meaning, unless we adopt a view of man that focuses on the will to meaning as his motivation?

What is revolutionary, however, is not only logotherapy's concept of the will to meaning, but also its concept of meaning in life. Indeed, logotherapists have broken a taboo: in a novel by Nicholas Mosley, the author writes, "There is a subject nowadays which is taboo in the way that sexuality was once taboo; which is to talk about life as if it had any meaning."[7] Logotherapists venture to talk about life as something that always has meaning. It goes without saying that this is mandatory in cases of noogenic neurosis or, for that matter, existential frustration. Here, logotherapy lends itself as specific therapy or, to couch it in professionally medical terms, as "the method of choice."

And then there is the question of determining treatment in a particular case. I am not weary of stating that the method of choice in each given instance boils down to an equation with two unknowns:

$$\psi = x + y$$

x stands for the unique personality of the patient and y for the equally unique personality of the therapist. In other words, not each and every method is applicable to each and every patient with the same success, nor is each and every therapist capable of handling each and every method with equal success. As to adjusting the method to the patient, the great psychiatrist Beard once said: "If you have treated 2 cases of neurasthenia in the same way, you have mistreated at least one of them." And as to adjusting the method to the therapist, another classic once said when he spoke of the method that he had introduced into psychiatry: "This technique has proved to be the only method suited to my individuality; I do not venture to deny that a physician quite differently might feel impelled to adopt a differ-

[7]Nicholas Mosley, *Natalie Natalia*, New York, Coward, McCann and Geoghegan.

ent attitude to his patients and the task before him." The man who said this was Sigmund Freud.[8]

Logotherapy cannot become too individualized. Method must be modified from person to person and also from situation to situation. Logotherapists must not only individualize but improvise. These skills can be learned by therapists, preferably by case demonstrations in the classroom setting, but also via publications. Believe me, among the best logotherapists from all over the world, there are some whom I have never met, nor have I been in correspondence with them. And they have turned out publications on their successful application of logotherapy, having based their work solely on reading my books! There are even people who managed to apply logotherapy with much success on themselves, also just after reading a book on the subject. They deserve to be commended on their creation, which one may call auto-biblio-logotherapy.

From whatever I have said before, it follows that logotherapy is no panacea. And from this again it follows that logotherapy is not only "open toward cooperation with other schools," but also its combination with other techniques should be encouraged and welcomed. That way, its effectiveness can be enlarged and expanded. And maybe Anatole Broyard[9] was right when he said in a review of one of my books, "If 'shrink' is the slang term for the Freudian analyst, then the logotherapist ought to be called 'stretch.'" So let us stretch the reach of logotherapy. Better to say, let us continue doing so.

But methods are not the whole story. Psychotherapy is always more than mere technique, and it is so to the extent to which it necessarily must include an element of wisdom. Art and wisdom form a wholeness and unity wherein dichotomies such as that between technique and encounter disappear and dissolve. Such extremes form a viable basis for psychotherapeutic interventions only in exceptional situations. Usually, the psychotherapeutic treatment contains both ingredients, strategies on one hand, and on the other I–Thou relationships.

---

[8]Sigmund Freud, quoted from Sandoz Psychiatric Spectator, 2 (1).
[9]Anatole Broyard, *The New York Times*, November 26, 1975.

An American girl,[10] a student of music, came to see me in Vienna for analysis. Since she spoke a terrible slang of which I could not understand a word, I tried to turn her over to an American physician in order to have him find out for me what had motivated her to seek my advice. She did not consult him, however, and when we happened to meet each other on the street, she explained: "See, Doctor, as soon as I had spoken to you of my problem, I felt such a relief that I didn't need help any longer." So I do not know even now why she had come to me.

At the other extreme is the following story.[11] In 1941, I was called one morning by the Gestapo and ordered to come to headquarters. I went there in the expectation of being immediately taken to a concentration camp. A Gestapo man was waiting for me in one of the offices; he started involving me in a cross-examination. But soon he changed the subject and began to question me on topics such as: What is psychotherapy? What is a neurosis? How would one treat a case of phobia? Then he began to elaborate on a specific case—the case of "his friend." Meanwhile, I had guessed that it was his own case that he wished to discuss with me. I started short-term therapy (more specifically, I applied the logotherapeutic technique of paradoxical intention); I advised him to tell "his friend" that he should do thus and so in case anxiety cropped up. This therapeutic session was not based on an I–Thou relation, but rather on one of I–he. The Gestapo man kept me for hours, and I continued treating him in this indirect manner. What effect this short-term therapy had I was, naturally, not able to discover. As for my family and myself, it was lifesaving for the moment, for we were permitted to stay in Vienna for a year before being sent to a concentration camp.

What I want to convey is that techniques must not be dismissed disparagingly. As to the logotherapeutic technique of paradoxical intention, however, L. Michael Ascher may be right

---

[10]Viktor E. Frankl, *Psychotherapy and Existentialism: Selected Papers on Logotherapy*, New York, Touchstone, 1978.
[11]Ibid.

in referring to it as something unique: "Most therapeutic approaches have specific techniques, and these techniques are not especially useful for, nor relevant to, alternative therapeutic systems. But there is one notable exception in this observation, namely, paradoxical intention. It is an exception because many professionals representing this wide variety of disparate approaches to psychotherapy have incorporated this intervention into their systems both practically and theoretically.[12]

I do not object to such "incorporations." After all, logotherapists do not treat patients *"ad maiorem gloriam logotherapiae,"* for the sake of enhancing the reputation of logotherapy, but for the benefit of the patients.

But now, rather than look forward, into the future of logotherapy, let us look back into its past. It turns out that Earnest Haeckel's biogenetic law, according to which ontogenesis is an abridged version of phylogenesis, also holds true of logotherapy, "the 3rd school of Viennese psychotherapy," as some authors call it. I was affiliated, one way or another, with the Freudian and Adlerian schools. As a high school student I corresponded with Sigmund Freud, and as a medical student, I met him. As early as 1924, a paper of mine was published by him in his *International Journal of Psychoanalysis*, and no more than one year later, in 1925, I published a paper in Alfred Adler's *International Journal of Individual Psychology*. To be sure, two years later he insisted on my being expelled from the Adlerian school—I had been too unorthodox.

But what about the contention that each founder of a psychotherapeutic school in the final analysis describes in his system his own neurosis and writes in his books his own case history? Of course, I am not entitled to speak, in this context, of Freud or Adler, but as far as logotherapy is concerned, I readily confess that as a young man I had to go through the hell of despair over the apparent meaninglessness of life, through total and ultimate nihilism, until I could develop an immunity against nihilism. I

[12] L. Michael Ascher, "Paradoxical Intention," *Handbook of Behavior Interventions,* A. Goldstein and E.B. Foa, eds., New York, Wiley, 1980.

developed logotherapy. It is a pity that other authors, instead of immunizing their readers against nihilism, innoculate them with their own cynicism, which is a defense mechanism, or reaction formation, that they have built up against their own nihilism.[13]

It is a pity, because today more than ever the despair over the apparent meaninglessness of life has become an urgent and topical issue on a worldwide scale. Our industrial society is out to satisfy each and every need, and our consumer society even creates some needs in order to satisfy them. The most important need, however, the basic need for meaning, remains—more often than not—ignored and neglected. And it is so "important" because once a man's will to meaning is fulfilled, he becomes able and capable of suffering, of coping with frustrations and tensions, and—if need be—he is prepared to give his life. Just look at the various political resistance movements throughout history and in present time. On the other hand, if man's will to meaning is frustrated, he is equally inclined to take his life, and he does so in the midst, and in spite, of all the welfare and affluence surrounding him. Just look at the staggering suicide figures in typical welfare states such as Sweden and Austria.

A decade ago, *The American Journal of Psychiatry*, when reviewing a book of mine, characterized the message of logotherapy as the "unconditional faith in an unconditional meaning" and asked the question, "What could be more pertinent as we enter 1970?" Now, in the midst of the 80s, Arthur G. Wirth[14] expresses his belief that "logotherapy has special relevance during this critical transition," by which he means the transition to "a post-petroleum society." In fact, I believe that crises such as the energy shortage present not only hazards, but also chances. They may be incentives to shift the accent and emphasis from mere means to meanings, from material goods to existential

[13]Viktor E. Frankl, *The Unheard Cry for Meaning: Psychotherapy and Humanism*, New York, Touchstone, 1979.

[14]Arthur G. Wirth, "Logotherapy and Education in a Post-Petroleum Society," *The International Forum for Logotherapy* 2 (3), 1980, 29–32.

needs. There is an energy shortage. But life can never become short of meaning. If there is, as some authors contend, anything such as a "logotherapeutic movement," it certainly belongs to the human rights movements. It focuses on the human right to a life as meaningful as possible.

I concluded my first book with the sentence that logotherapy "is a no-man's land. And yet—what a land of promise!" This was many years ago. In the meantime, the "no-man's land" has become inhabited. And the works of its population prove also that the "promise" is on the way to being fulfilled.

APPENDICES

🌿 🌿 🌿

SELECTED
ENGLISH-LANGUAGE
BIBLIOGRAPHY OF LOGOTHERAPY

1. Books

Bulka, Reuven P., *The Quest for Ultimate Meaning: Principles and Applications of Logotherapy.* Foreword by Viktor E. Frankl. New York, Philosophical Library, 1979.

Crumbaugh, James C., *Everything to Gain: A Guide to Self-fulfillment Through Logoanalysis.* Chicago, Nelson-Hall, 1973.

Crumbaugh, James C., William M. Wood, and W. Chadwick Wood, *Logotherapy: New Help for Problem Drinkers.* Foreword by Viktor E. Frankl. Chicago, Nelson-Hall, 1980.

Fabry, Joseph B., *The Pursuit of Meaning: Viktor Frankl, Logotherapy, and Life.* Preface by Viktor E. Frankl. Boston, Beacon Press, 1968; New York, Harper & Row, 1980.

Fabry, Joseph B., Reuven P. Bulka, and William S. Sahakian, eds., *Logotherapy in Action.* Foreword by Viktor E. Frankl. New York, Jason Aronson, Inc., 1979.

Frankl, Viktor E., *The Doctor and the Soul: From Psychotherapy to Logotherapy.* New York, Alfred A. Knopf, Inc.; second, expanded edition, 1965; paperback edition, New York, Vintage Books, 1986.

Frankl, Viktor E., *Man's Search for Meaning: An Introduction to Logotherapy.* Preface by Gordon W. Allport. Boston, Beacon Press, 1959; paperback edition, New York, Pocket Books, 1987.

Frankl, Viktor E., *Psychotherapy and Existentialism: Selected Papers on Logotherapy.* New York, Washington Square Press, 1985.

Frankl, Viktor E., *The Will to Meaning: Foundations and Applications of Logotherapy.* New York and Cleveland, The World Publishing Company, 1969; paperback edition, New York, New American Library, 1981.

Frankl, Viktor E., *The Unconscious God: Psychotherapy and Theology.* New York, Simon and Schuster, 1985.

Frankl, Viktor E., *The Unheard Cry for Meaning: Psychotherapy and Humanism.* New York, Simon and Schuster, 1985.

Frankl, Viktor E., *Synchronization in Buchenwald*, a play, offset, $5.00 (with an introductory audiotape $9.00). Available at the Institute of Logotherapy, P.O. Box 2852, Saratoga, CA 95070.

Jones, Frederic H., and Judith K. Jones, *Viktor Frankl's Logotherapy. The Proceedings of the Fifth World Congress of Logotherapy.* Berkeley, Institute of Logotherapy Press, 1986.

Lazar, Edward, Sandra A. Wawrytko, and James W. Kidd, eds., *Viktor Frankl, People and Meaning: A Commemorative Tribute to the Founder of Logotherapy on His Eightieth Birthday.* San Francisco, Golden Phoenix Press, 1985.

Leslie, Robert C., *Jesus and Logotherapy: The Ministry of Jesus as Interpreted Through the Psychotherapy of Viktor Frankl.* New York and Nashville, Abingdon Press, 1965; paperback edition, 1968.

Lukas, Elisabeth, *Meaningful Living. Logotherapeutic Guide to Health.* Foreword by Viktor E. Frankl. New York, Grove Press, 1986.

Lukas, Elisabeth, *Meaning in Suffering: Comfort in Crisis Through Logotherapy.* Berkeley, Institute of Logotherapy Press, 1986.

Takashima, Hiroshi, *Psychomatic Medicine and Logotherapy.* Foreword by Viktor E. Frankl. Oceanside, New York, Dabor Science Publications, 1977.

Takashima, Hiroshi, *Humanistic Psychosomatic Medicine. A Logotherapy Book.* Berkeley, Institute of Logotherapy Press, 1985.

Tweedie, Donald F., *Logotherapy and the Christian Faith: An Evaluation of Frankl's Existential Approach to Psychotherapy.* Preface by Viktor E. Frankl. Grand Rapids, Baker Book House, 1961; paperback edition, 1972.

Tweedie, Donald F., *The Christian and the Couch: An Introduction to Christian Logotherapy.* Grand Rapids, Baker Book House, 1963.

Ungersma, Aaron J., *The Search for Meaning: A New Approach in Psychotherapy and Pastoral Psychology.* Philadelphia, Westminster Press, 1961; paperback edition, Foreword by Viktor E. Frankl, 1968.

Wawrytko, Sandra A., ed., *Analecta Frankliana: The Proceedings of the First World Congress of Logotherapy (1980).* Berkeley, Institute of Logotherapy Press, 1982.

2. *Chapters in Books*

Ascher, L. Michael, "Paradoxical Intention," in *Handbook of Behavioral Interventions*, A. Goldstein and E. B. Foa, eds. New York, John Wiley, 1980.

Ascher, L. Michael, and C. Alex Pollard, "Paradoxical Intention," in *The Therapeutic Efficacy of the Major Psychotherapeutic Techniques*, Usuf Hariman, ed., Springfield, Charles C. Thomas, 1983.

Ascher, L. Michael, Michael R. Bowers, and David E. Schotte, "A Review of Data from Controlled Case Studies and Experiments Evaluating the Clinical Efficacy of Paradoxical Intention," in *Promoting Change Through Paradoxical Therapy*, Gerald R. Weeks, ed. Homewood, IL, Dow Jones-Irwin, 1985, pp. 99–110.

Ascher, L. Michael, and Robert A. DiTomasso, "Paradoxical Intention in Behavior Therapy: A Review of the Experimental Literature," in *Evaluating Behavior Therapy Outcome*, Ralph McMillan Turner and L. Michael Ascher, eds. New York, Springer, 1985.

Frankl, Viktor E., "The Philosophical Foundations of Logotherapy" (paper read before the first Lexington Conference on Phenomenology on April 4, 1963), in *Phenomenology: Pure and Applied*, Erwin Straus, ed. Pittsburgh, Duquesne University Press, 1964.

Frankl, Viktor E., "Reductionism and Nihilism," in *Beyond Reductionism: New Perspectives in the Life Sciences* (The Alpbach Symposium, 1968), Arthur Koestler and J. R. Smythies, eds. New York, Macmillan, 1970.

Frankl, Viktor E., "Man's Search for Ultimate Meaning," in *On the Way to Self-Knowledge*, Jacob Needleman, ed. New York, Alfred A. Knopf, Inc., 1976.

Frankl, Viktor E., "Logotherapy," in *The Psychotherapy Handbook*, Richie Herink, ed. New York, New American Library, 1980.

Frankl, Viktor E., "Opening Address to the First World Congress of Logotherapy: Logotherapy on Its Way to Degurufication," in *Analecta Frankliana: The Proceedings of the First World Congress of Logotherapy (1980)*, Sandra A. Wawrytko, ed., Berkeley, Institute of Logotherapy Press, 1982.

Frankl, Viktor E., "Logotherapy," in *Encyclopedia of Psychology*, Raymond J. Corsini, ed. Volume 2. New York, John Wiley, 1984.

Frankl, Viktor E., "Paradoxical Intention," in *Promoting Change Through Paradoxical Therapy*, Gerald R. Weeks, ed. Homewood, IL, Dow Jones-Irwin, 1985.

Frankl, Viktor E., "Logos, Paradox, and the Search for Meaning," in *Cognition and Psychotherapy*, Michael J. Mahoney and Arthur Freeman, eds. New York, Plenum Press, 1985.

Marks, Isaac M., "Paradoxical Intention ('Logotherapy')," in *Fears and Phobias*. New York, Academic Press, 1969.

Marks, Isaac M., "Paradoxical Intention," in *Behavior Modification*, W. Stewart Agras, ed. Boston, Little, Brown and Company, 1972.

Marks, Isaac M., "Paradoxical Intention (Logotherapy)," in *Encyclopaedic Handbook of Medical Psychology*, Stephen Krauss, ed. London and Boston, Butterworth, 1976.

Maslow, Abraham H., "Comments on Dr. Frankl's Paper," in *Readings in Humanistic Psychology*, Anthony J. Sutich and Miles A. Vich, eds. New York, The Free Press, 1969.

Sahakian, William S., "Viktor Frankl," in *History of Psychology*. Itasca, IL, F. E. Peacock Publishers, Inc., 1968.

Schultz, Duane P., "The Self-Transcendent Person: Frankl's Model," in *Growth Psychology: Models of the Healthy Personality*. New York, Van Nostrand Reinhold, 1977.

Schultz, Duane P., "Frankl's Model of the Self-Transcendent Person," in *Psychology in Use: An Introduction to Applied Psychology*. New York, Macmillan, 1979.

Seltzer, Leon F., "Paradoxical Intention," in *Paradoxical Strategies in Psychotherapy*, New York, John Wiley, 1986.

Spiegelberg, Herbert, "Viktor Frankl: Phenomenology in Logotherapy and Existenzanalyse," in *Phenomenology in Psychology and Psychiatry*. Evanston, IL, Northwestern University Press, 1972.

Weeks, Gerald R., and Luciano L'Abate, "Research on Paradoxical Intention," in *Paradoxical Psychotherapy*. New York, Brunner/Mazel, 1982.

Williams, David A., and Joseph Fabry, "The Existential Approach: Logotherapy," in *Basic Approaches to Group Psychotherapy and Group Counseling*, George M. Gazda, ed., Springfield, Charles C. Thomas, 1982.

3. Articles and Miscellaneous

Addad, Moshe, "Psychogenic Neuroticism and Noogenic Self-Strengthening." *The International Forum for Logotherapy*, Volume 10, Number 1, Spring-Summer 1987, 52–59.

Ansbacher, Rowena R., "The Third Viennese School of Psychotherapy." *Journal of Individual Psychology*, XV 1959, 236–37.

Ascher, L. Michael, "Employing Paradoxical Intention in the Behavioral Treatment of Urinary Retention." *Scandinavian Journal of Behavior Therapy*, Volume 6, Supplement 4, 1977, 28.

Ascher, L. Michael, "Paradoxical Intention: A Review of Preliminary Research." *The International Forum for Logotherapy*, Volume 1, Number 1, Winter 1978–Spring 1979, 18–21.

Ascher, L. Michael, "Paradoxical intention in the treatment of urinary retention." *Behavior Research & Therapy*, Volume 17, 1979, 267–270.

Ascher, L. Michael, "Paradoxical Intention Viewed by a Behavior Therapist." *The International Forum for Logotherapy*, Volume 2, Number 3, Spring 1980, 13–16.

Ascher, L. Michael, "Application of Paradoxical Intention by Other Schools of Therapy." *The International Forum for Logotherapy*, Volume 4, Number 1, Spring-Summer 1981, 52–55.

Ascher, L. Michael, "Employing paradoxical intention in the treatment of agoraphobia." *Behavior Research & Therapy*, 19, 1981, 533–542.

Ascher, L. Michael, and Jay S. Efran, "Use of Paradoxical Intention in a Behavior Program for Sleep Onset Insomnia." *Journal of Consulting and Clinical Psychology*, 46, 1978, 547–550.

Ascher, L. Michael, David E. Schotte, and John B. Grayson, "Enhancing Effectiveness of Paradoxical Intention in Treating Travel Restriction in Agoraphobia." *Behavior Therapy* 17, 1986, 124–130.

Ascher, L. Michael, and Ralph MacMillan Turner, "Paradoxical Intention and Insomnia: An Experimental Investigation." *Behavior Research & Therapy*, Volume 17, 1979, 408–411.

Ascher, L. Michael, and Ralph MacMillan Turner, "A comparison of two methods for the administration of paradoxical intention." *Behavior Research & Therapy*, Volume 18, 1980, 121–126.

Boeringa, J. Alexander, "Blushing: A Modified Behavioral Intervention Using Pardoxical Intention." *Psychotherapy: Theory, Research and Practice*, Volume 20, Number 4, Winter 1983, 441–444.

Carter, Robert E., "The Ground of Meaning: Logotherapy, Psychotherapy, and Kohlberg's Developmentalism." *The International Forum for Logotherapy*, Volume 9, Number 2, Fall-Winter 1986, 116–124.

Chakravarti, Sitansu S., "Hinduism and Logotherapy." *The International Forum for Logotherapy*, Volume 10, Number 1, Spring-Summer 1987, 44–45.

Cohen, David, "The Frankl Meaning." *Human Behavior*, Volume 6, Number 7, July 1977, 56–62.

Crumbaugh, James C., "The Seeking of Noetic Goals Test (SONG): A Complementary Scale to the Purpose in Life Test (PIL)." *Journal of Clinical Psychology*, July 1977, Volume 33, Number 3, 900–907.

Crumbaugh, James C., and Leonard T. Maholick, "An Experimental Study in Existentialism: The Psychometric Approach to Frankl's Concept of Noogenic Neurosis." *Journal of Clinical Psychology*, XX, 1964, 200–207.

Dansart, Bernard, "Development of a Scale to Measure Attitudinal Values as Defined by Viktor Frankl." Dissertation, Northern Illinois University, De Kalb, 1974.

"The Doctor and the Soul: Dr. Viktor Frankl." *Harvard Medical Alumni Bulletin*, XXXVI, Number 1, Fall 1961, 8.

Eisner, Harry R., "Purpose in Life as a Function of Locus of Control and Attitudinal Values: a Test of Two of Viktor Frankl's Concepts." Dissertation, Marquette University, 1978.

Eng, Erling, "The Akedah, Oedipus, and Dr. Frankl." *Psychotherapy: Theory, Research and Practice*, Volume 16, Number 3, Fall 1979, 269–271.

Fabry, Joseph, "Some Practical Hints About Paradoxical Intention." *The International Forum for Logotherapy*, Volume 5, Number 1, Spring-Summer 1982, 25–30.

Finck, Willis C., "The Viktor E. Frankl Merit Award." *The International Forum for Logotherapy*, Volume 5, Number 2, Fall-Winter 1982, 73.

Frankl, Viktor E., "Logos and Existence in Psychotherapy." *American Journal of Psychotherapy*, VII, 1953, 8–15.

Frankl, Viktor E., "The Concept of Man in Psychotherapy" (paper read before the Royal Society of Medicine, Section of Psychiatry, London, England, June 15, 1954). *Pastoral Psychology*, VI, 1955, 16–26.

Frankl, Viktor E., "On Logotherapy and Existential Analysis" (paper read before the Association for the Advancement of Psychoanalysis, New York, April 19, 1957). *American Journal of Psychoanalysis*, XVIII, 1958, 28–37.

Frankl, Viktor E., "The Search for Meaning." *Saturday Review* September 13, 1958.

Frankl, Viktor E., "The Spiritual Dimension in Existential Analysis and Logotherapy" (paper read before the Fourth International Congress of Psychotherapy, Barcelona, September 5, 1958). *Journal of Individual Psychology*, XV, 1959, 157–65.

Frankl, Viktor E., "Paradoxical Intention: A Logotherapeutic Technique" (paper read before the American Association for the Advancement of Psychotherapy, New York, February 26, 1960). *American Journal of Psychotherapy*, XIV, 1960, 520–35.

Frankl, Viktor E., "Logotherapy and Existential Analysis: A Review" (paper read before the Symposium on Logotherapy, 6th International Congress of Psychotherapy, London, August 26, 1964). *American Journal of Psychotherapy*, XX, 1966, 252–60.

Frankl, Viktor E., "Logotherapy." *The Israel Annals of Psychiatry and Related Disciplines*, VII, 1967, 142–55.

Frankl, Viktor E., "The Feeling of Meaninglessness: A Challenge to Psychotherapy." *The American Journal of Psychoanalysis*, XXXII, Number 1, 1972, 85–89.

Frankl, Viktor E., "Encounter: The Concept and Its Vulgarization." *The Journal of the American Academy of Psychoanalysis*, I, Number 1, 1973, 73–83.

Frankl, Viktor E., "Endogenous Depression and Noogenic Neurosis." *The International Forum for Logotherapy*, Volume 2, Number 2, Summer-Fall, 1979, 38–40.

Frankl, Viktor E., "Psychotherapy on Its Way to Rehumanization." *The International Forum for Logotherapy*, Volume 3, Number 2, Fall 1980, 3–9.

Frankl, Viktor E., "The Future of Logotherapy." *The International Forum for Logotherapy*, Volume 4, Number 2, Fall-Winter 1981, 71–78.

Frankl, Viktor E., "The Meaning Crisis in the First World and Hunger in the Third World." *The International Forum for Logotherapy*, Volume 7, Number 1, Spring-Summer 1984, 5–7.

Frankl, Viktor E., "Science, Man and Meaning" (Opening lecture at the 8th International Congress on Fibrinolysis, Vienna, August 25–29, 1986). *Fibrinolysis* (1987) 1, 13–16.

Frankl, Viktor E. "On the Meaning of Love." *The International Forum for Logotherapy*, Volume 10, Number 1, Spring-Summer 1987, 5–8.

Garfield, Charles A., "A Psychometric and Clinical Investigation of Frankl's Concept of Existential Vacuum and of Anomie." *Psychiatry*, XXXVI, 1973, 396–408.

Gerz, Hans O., "The Treatment of the Phobic and the Obsessive-Compulsive Patient Using Paradoxical Intention sec. Viktor E. Frankl." *Journal of Neuropsychiatry*, III, Number 6, July–August 1962, 375–87.

Gerz, Hans O., "Experience with the Logotherapeutic Technique of Paradoxical Intention in the Treatment of Phobic and Obsessive-Compulsive Patients" (paper read at the Symposium of Logotherapy at the 6th International Congress of Psychotherapy, London, August 1964). *American Journal of Psychiatry*, CXXIII, Number 5, November 1966, 548–53.

Giorgi, Bruno, "The Belfast Test: A New Psychometric Approach to Logotherapy." *The International Forum for Logotherapy*, Volume 5, Number 1, Spring-Summer 1982, 31–37.

Greenberg, R. P., and R. Pies, "Is paradoxical intention risk-free?" *Journal of Clinical Psychiatry* 44, 1983, 66–69.

Hall, Mary Harrington, "A Conversation with Viktor Frankl of Vienna." *Psychology Today*, I, Number 9, February 1968, 56–63.

Hatcher, Gordon, "A Study of Viktor E. Frankl's and Karl A. Menninger's Concepts of Love." Dissertation, University of the Pacific, Stockton, California, 1968.

Havens, Leston L., "Paradoxical Intention." *Psychiatry and Social Science Review*, II, 1968, 16–19.

Holmes, R. M., "Meaning and Responsibility: A Comparative Analysis of the Concept of the Responsible Self in Search of Meaning in the Thought of Viktor Frankl and H. Richard Niebuhr with Certain Implications for the Church's Ministry to the University." Doctoral dissertation, Pacific School of Religion, Berkeley, California, 1965.

Hsu, L. K. George, and Stuart Lieberman, "Paradoxical Intention in the Treatment of Chronic Anorexia Nervosa." *American Journal of Psychiatry* 139, 1982, 650–653.

Hutzell, Robert R., and Thomas J. Peterson, "An MMPI Existential Vacuum Scale for Logotherapy Research." *The International*

Forum for Logotherapy, Volume 8, Number 2, Fall-Winter 1985, 97–100.

Hyman, William, "Practical Aspects of Logotherapy in Neurosurgery." *Existential Psychiatry*, VIII, 1969, 99–101.

Kaczanowski, Godfryd, "Frankl's Logotherapy." *American Journal of Psychiatry*, CXVII, 1960, 563.

Kalmar, Stephen S., "The Viktor E. Frankl Scholarship 1983." *The International Forum for Logotherapy*, Volume 6, Number 2, Fall-Winter 1983, 84–85.

Klapper, Naomi, "On Being Human: A Comparative Study of Abraham J. Heschel and Viktor Frankl." Doctoral dissertation, Jewish Theological Seminary of America, New York, 1973.

Kovacs, George, "The Philosophy of Death in Viktor E. Frankl." *Journal of Phenomenological Psychology*, Volume 13, Number 2, Fall 1982, 197–209.

Kovacs, George, "Viktor E. Frankl's place in Philosophy." *The International Forum for Logotherapy*, Volume 8, Number 1, Spring-Summer 1985, 17–21.

Ladouceur, R., and Y. Gros-Louis: "Paradoxical intention vs. stimulus control in the treatment of severe insomnia." *Journal of Behavior Therapy and Experimental Psychiatry* 17, 1986, 267–269.

Lamb, C. S., "The use of paradoxical intention: Self-management through laughter." *Personal and Guidance Journal*, 59, 1980, 217–219.

Lamontagne, Ives, "Treatment of Erythrophobia by Paradoxical Intention." *The Journal of Nervous and Mental Disease*, Volume 166, Number 4, 1978, 304–306.

Lantz, James E., "Dereflection in Family Therapy with Schizophrenic Clients." *The International Forum for Logotherapy*, Volume 5, Number 2, Fall-Winter 1982, 119–122.

Lantz, James, "Family Logotherapy." *Contemporary Family Therapy*, 8, 1986, 124–135.

Lantz, James, "Franklian Family Therapy." *The International Forum for Logotherapy*, Volume 10, Number 1, Spring-Summer 1987, 22–28.

Lantz, James, and John Belcher, "Schizophrenia and the Existential Vacuum." *The International Forum for Logotherapy*, Volume 10, Number 1, Spring-Summer 1987, 17–21.

Lazar, Edward, "Logotherapeutic Support Groups for Cardiac Patients." *The International Forum for Logotherapy*, Volume 7, Number 2, Fall-Winter 1984, pp. 85–88

Leslie, Robert C., "Viktor Frankl and C. G. Jung." *Shiggaion*, Volume X, Number 2, December 1961.

Levinson, Jay Irwin, "A Combination of Paradoxical Intention and Dereflection," *The International Forum for Logotherapy*, Volume 2, Number 2, Summer-Fall 1979, 40–41.

Lukas, Elisabeth S., "New Ways for Dereflection." *The International Forum for Logotherapy*, Volume 4, Number 1, Spring-Summer, 1981, 13–28.

Lukas, Elisabeth S., "Validation of Logotherapy." *The International Forum for Logotherapy*, Volume 4, Number 2, Fall-Winter 1981, 116–125.

Lukas, Elisabeth, "The 'Birthmarks' of Paradoxical Intention." *The International Forum for Logotherapy*, Volume 5, Number 1, Spring-Summer 1982, 20–24.

Lukas, Elisabeth, "Logotherapy: Healing through Meaning." *The International Forum for Logotherapy*, Volume 10, Number 1 Spring-Summer 1987, 9–16.

Mahoney, Michael J., "Paradoxical Intention, Symptom Prescription, and Principles of Therapeutic Change." *The Counseling Psychologist*, Volume 4, Number 2, April 1986, 283–290.

Maslow, A. H., "Comments on Dr. Frankl's Paper." *Journal of Humanistic Psychology*, VI, 1966, 107–12.

Mavissakalian, M., Michelson, L., D. Greenwald, S. Kornblith, and M. Greenwald, "Cognitive-behavioral treatment of agoraphobia: Paradoxical intention vs. self-statement training." *Behavior Research & Therapy*, 1983, 21, 75–86.

"Meaning in Life." *Time*, February 2, 1968, 38–40.

Meier, Augustine, "Frankl's 'Will to Meaning' as Measured by the Purpose-in-Life Test in Relation to Age and Sex Differences." *Journal of Clinical Psychology*, XXX, 1974, 384–86.

Michelson, L., and M. A. Ascher, "Paradoxical Intention in the treatment of agoraphobia and other anxiety disorders." *J. Behav. Ther. Exp. Psychiatry* 15, 1984, 215–220.

Milan, M. A., and D. J. Kolko, "Paradoxical intention in the treatment of obsessional flatulence ruminations." *J. Behav. Ther. Exp. Psychiatry*, XIII, 1982, 167–172.

Minton, Gary, "A Comparative Study of the Concept of Conscience in the Writings of Sigmund Freud and Viktor Frankl." Dissertation, New Orleans Baptist Theological Seminary, 1967.

Murphy, Leonard: "Extent of Purpose-in-Life and Four Frankl Proposed Life Objectives." Doctoral dissertation in Department of Psychology, University of Ottawa, 1967.

Nackord, Ernest J., Jr., "A College Test of Logotherapeutic Concepts." *The International Forum for Logotherapy*, Volume 6, Number 2, Fall-Winter 1983, 117–122.

Newton, Joseph R., "Therapeutic Paradoxes, Paradoxical Intentions, and Negative Practice." *American Journal of Psychotherapy*, XXII, 1968, 68–81.

Noonan, J. Robert, "A Note on an Eastern Counterpart of Frankl's Paradoxical Intention." *Psychologia*, XII, 1969, 147–49.

O'Connell, Walter E., "Viktor Frankl, the Adlerian?" *Psychiatric Spectator*, Volume VI, Number 11, 1970, 13–14.

Okechukwu Iwundu, Charles, "Pedagogy and Logotherapy." *The International Forum for Logotherapy*, Volume 10, Number 1, Spring-Summer 1987, 60–62.

Ott, B. D., "The efficacy of paradoxical intention in the treatment of sleep onset insomnia under differential feedback conditions." Dissertation, Hofstra University, 1980.

Ott, B.D., B.A., Levine, and L.M. Ascher, "Manipulating the explicit demand of paradoxical intention instructions." *Behavioural Psychotherapy*, 1983, 11, 25–35.

Porter, Jack Nusan, "The Affirmation of Life After the Holocaust: The Contributions of Bettelheim, Lifton and Frankl." *The Association for Humanistic Psychology Newsletter*, August-September 1980, 9–11.

Relinger, Helmut, Philip H. Bornstein, and Dan M. Mungas, "Treatment of Insomnia by Paradoxical Intention: A Time-Series Analysis." *Behavior Therapy*, Volume 9, 1978, 955–959.

Sargent, George A., "Combining Paradoxical Intention with Behavior Modification." *The International Forum for Logotherapy*, Volume 6, Number 1, Spring-Summer 1983, 28–30.

Schachter, Stanley J., "Bettelheim and Frankl: Contradicting Views of the Holocaust." *Reconstructionist*, XXVI, Number 20 (February 10, 1961), 6–11.

Solyom, L., J. Garza-Perez, B. L. Ledwidge, and C. Solyom, "Paradoxical Intention in the Treatment of Obsessive Thoughts: A Pilot Study." *Comprehensive Psychiatry*, Volume 13, Number 3, May 1972, 291–97.

Thompson, Yaakov, "A Question of Meaning: Rabbinical Counseling and Logotherapeutic Models." *The International Forum for Logotherapy*, Volume 10, Number 1, Spring-Summer 1987, 29–34.

Timms, M.W.H., "Treatment of chronic blushing by paradoxical intention." *Behavioral Psychotherapy* 89, 1980, 59–61.

Turner, Ralph M., and L. Michael Ascher, "Controlled Comparison of Progressive Relaxation, Stimulus Control, and Paradoxical Intention Therapies for Insomnia." *Journal of Consulting and Clinical Psychology*, Volume 47, Number 3, 1979, 500–508.

Victor, Ralph G., and Carolyn M. Krug, "Paradoxical Intention in the Treatment of Compulsive Gambling." *American Journal of Psychotherapy*, XXI, Number 4, October 1967, 808–14.

Waugh, Robert J.L., "Paradoxical Intention." *American Journal of Psychiatry*, Volume 123, Number 10, April 1967, 1305–1306.

Yoder, James D., "A Child, Paradoxical Intention, and Consciousness." *The International Forum for Logotherapy*, Volume 6, Number 1, Spring-Summer 1983, 19–21.

4. Films, Records, and Tapes

Frankl, Viktor E., "Frankl and the Search for Meaning," a film produced by Psychological Films, 110 North Wheeler Street, Orange, CA 92669.

Frankl, Viktor E., "The Rehumanization of Psychotherapy. A Workshop Sponsored by the Division of Psychotherapy of the American Psychological Association," a videotape. Address inquiries to Division of Psychotherapy, American Psychological Association, 1220 Seventeenth Street, N.W., Washington, DC 20036.

Frankl, Viktor E., "Human Freedom and Meaning in Life" and "Self-Transcendence—Therapeutic Agent in Sexual Neurosis," videotapes. Copies of the tapes can be ordered for a service fee. Address inquiries to the Manager, Learning Resource Distribution Center, United States International University, San Diego, CA 92131.

Frankl, Viktor E., Two 5-hour lectures, part of the course Human Behavior 616, "Man in Search of Meaning," during the winter quarter, 1976. Copies of the videotapes can be ordered for a service fee. Address inquiries to the Manager, Learning Resource Distribution Center, United States International University, San Diego, CA 92131.

Frankl, Viktor E., "A panel of experts from the fields of medicine, anthropology, psychiatry, religion, social work, philosophy, and clinical psychology, discussing topics of interest with Dr. Frankl at the First World Congress of Logotherapy, San Diego, 1980." A 51-minute videotape. $53.00. Make check payable to the Institute of Logotherapy, P.O. Box 2852, Saratoga, CA 95070. When ordering, state kind of tape wanted (Beta, VHS, or ¾" U-matic).

Frankl, Viktor E.: "The Meaning of Suffering," a lecture given on January 31, 1983. Available for rental or purchase from Health Science Information Center, Cedars-Sinai Medical Center, 8700 Beverly Blvd., Los Angeles, CA 90048. Audiocassette, $15.00. Videocassette, $50.00.

Frankl, Viktor E., "The Will to Meaning," a public lecture recorded at Dallas Brooks Hall, Melbourne (July 21st, 1985). A Videocassette ($75.00). Address inquiries to the Viktor Frankl Committee, P.O. Box 321, Boronia, 3155, Australia.

Frankl, Viktor E., "Resources of Survival," a public lecture given at the University of South Africa in Pretoria on June 24, 1986. Videotapes (VHS and Beta) and audiotapes available from the University of South Africa, P.O. Box 392, 0001 Pretoria, Republic of South Africa.

Frankl, Viktor E., Lecture at the First Brazilian Congress of Logotherapy in Rio de Janeiro on October 18, 1986. Videotape available from the Centro de Psicologia Comunitaria, Caixa Postal 691, 13100 Campinas SP, Brasil. $60.00.

Frankl, Viktor E., A Conversation with Professor Richard Evans of the University of Houston. Videotape (VHS or Beta) available from the Institute of Logotherapy, P.O. Box 2852, Saratoga, CA 95070. $250.00.

Frankl, Viktor E., "The Rehumanization of Psychotherapy." (Address by Viktor E. Frankl in Texas when he received the John P. McGovern award.) Videotape (VHS or Beta) available from the Institute of Logotherapy, P.O. Box 2852, Saratoga, CA 95070, USA. $45.00.

Frankl, Viktor E., An Interview by Patricia L. Starck with Viktor E. Frankl and Jerry Long, Jr. Videotape (VHS or Beta) available from the Institute of Logotherapy, P.O. Box 2852, Saratoga, CA 95070. $35.00.

Frankl, Viktor E., "Resources of Survival," a lecture given at Southern Methodist University on November 12, 1987. Video-cassette available at the Department of SMU, 103 Fondren Library West, Dallas, Texas 75275. $40.00

Frankl, Viktor E., "Meaninglessness: Today's Dilemma," an audio-tape produced by Creative Resources, 4800 West Waco Drive, Waco, TX 76703.

Frankl, Viktor E., "Man's Search for Meaning. An Introduction to Logotherapy." Recording for the Blind, Inc., 215 East 58th Street, New York, NY 10022.

Frankl, Viktor E., "Youth in Search of Meaning." Word Cassette Library (WCL 0205), 4800 West Waco Drive, Waco, TX 76703 ($5.95).

Frankl, Viktor E., "Theory and Therapy of Neurosis: A Series of Lectures Delivered at the United States International University in San Diego, California." Eight 90-minute cassettes produced by Creative Resources, 4800 West Waco Drive, Waco, TX 76703 ($79.95).

Frankl, Viktor E., "Man in Search of Meaning: A Series of Lectures Delivered at the United States International University in San Diego, California." Fourteen 90-minute cassettes produced by Creative Resources, 4800 West Waco Drive, Waco, TX 76703 ($139.95).

Frankl, Viktor E., "The Neurotization of Humanity and the Rehumanization of Psychotherapy," two cassettes. Argus Communications, 7440 Natchez Avenue, Niles, IL 60648 ($14.00).

Frankl, Viktor E., "Therapy Through Meaning," Psychotherapy Tape Library (T 656), Post Graduate Center, 124 East 8th Street, New York, N.Y. 10016 ($15.00).

Frankl, Viktor E., "Existential Psychotherapy," two cassettes. The Center for Cassette Studies, 8110 Webb Avenue, North Hollywood, CA 91605.

Frankl, Viktor E., "The Defiant Power of the Human Spirit: A Message of Meaning in a Chaotic World." Address at the Berkeley Community Theater, November 2, 1979. A 90-minute cassette tape, $6.00. Available at the Institute of Logotherapy, P.O. Box 2852, Saratoga, CA 95070.

Frankl, Viktor E., "The Meaning of Suffering for the Terminally Ill" (International Seminar on Terminal Care, Montreal, October 8, 1980). Audio Transcripts, Ltd. (Code 25-107-80 A and B), P.O. Box 487, Times Square Station, New York, N.Y. 10036.

Frankl, Viktor E., "The Rehumanization of Psychotherapy," lecture on the occasion of the inauguration of the Logotherapy Counseling Center of Atlanta and Athens on November 14, 1980. Audiocassette (1/404/542-4766) available from the Center for Continuing Education, the University of Georgia, Athens, GA 30602.

Frankl, Victor E., "Man in Search of Ultimate Meaning," Oskar Pfister Award Lecture at the American Psychiatric Association's annual meeting (Dallas, 1985). Audiocassette (L 19-186-85) produced by Audio Transcripts, 610 Madison Street, Alexandria, Virginia 22314 ($10.00).

Frankl, Viktor E., "Man in Search of Meaning. The Philosophical Foundations of Logotherapy," a lecture given on November 22, 1986 at the Open Philosophical University, Bilthoven, The Netherlands. Audiocassette (3017-1186) available from Tekstotaal, P.O. Box 9264, 3506 GG Utrecht, The Netherlands. Price: USD 8.00.

Frankl, Viktor E., Robin W. Goodenough, Iver Hand, Oliver A. Phillips, and Edith Weisskopf-Joelson, "Logotherapy: Theory and Practice. A Symposium Sponsored by the Division of Psychotherapy of the American Psychological Association," an audiotape. Address inquiries to Division of Psychotherapy, American Psychological Association, 1200 Seventeenth Street, N.W., Washington, D.C. 20036.

Frankl, Viktor E., and Huston Smith, "Value Dimensions in Teaching," a color-television film produced by Hollywood Animators, Inc., for the California Junior College Association. Rental or purchase through Dr. Rex Wignall, Director, Chaffey College, Alta Loma, CA 91701.

"The Humanistic Revolution: Pioneers in Perspective," interviews with leading humanistic psychologists: Abraham Maslow, Gardner Murphy, Carl Rogers, Rollo May, Paul Tillich, Frederick Perls, Viktor Frankl and Alan Watts. Psychological Films, 110 North Wheeler Street, Orange, CA 92669. Sale $250; rental $20.

Leslie, Robert C., (moderator) with Joseph Fabry and Mary Ann Finch, "A Conversation with Viktor E. Frankl on Occasion of the Inauguration of the 'Frankl Library and Memorabilia' at the Graduate Theological Union on February 12, 1977," a videotape. Copies may be obtained from Professor Robert C. Leslie, 1798 Scenic Avenue, Berkeley, CA 94709.

5. Braille Editions

Fabry, Joseph B., *The Pursuit of Meaning: Logotherapy Applied to Life*. Available on loan at no cost from Woodside Terrace Kiwanis Braille Project, 850 Longview Road, Hillsborough, CA 94010.

Frankl, Viktor E., *Man's Search for Meaning: An Introduction to Logotherapy*. Available on loan at no cost from Woodside Terrace Kiwanis Braille Project, 850 Longview Road, Hillsborough, CA 94010.

Frankl, Viktor E., *The Unheard Cry for Meaning: Psychotherapy and Humanism*. Available on loan at no cost from Woodside Terrace Kiwanis Braille Project, 850 Longview Road, Hillsborough, CA 94010.

SUBJECT INDEX

Abyss–experience, 83
Adlerian psychology, 26, 34, 67
affluence, 47, 65
analysis, 9
anthropological dimension, 17, 22
anthropomorphism, 148–149
anticipatory anxiety, 102–103, 105
anxiety neurosis, 103
artist, 4

behaviorism, 26
behavior therapy, 26, 110, 116
being in the world, 3–4, 51, 162
belief, 92, 148

collective neurosis, 94
computor, 21
concentration camps, 78–79
concept of man, 15, 28
conformism, 65, 83
conscience, 18–19, 40–41, 57, 63 ff., 85, 143
contraindication, 114
corrugator phenomenon, 126

Dasein, 3
Daseinsanalyse, 5, 9

defense mechanism, 167
dereflection, 110–101, 115–116, 126
dialogue, 8, 118 ff., 124
dimensional anthropology and/or ontology, 22 ff., 27, 29, 74, 77–78, 88
dimensional difference, 145–146, 151
drug treatment, 28, 103, 110, 131
dynamics, 6, 112–113, 115–116, 124, 128, 138

education, 45–46, 64, 85–86, 136–137
electroconvulsive treatment, 28
encounter 6 ff., 11, 40, 69–70
endogenous depression, 114, 125–126
existential analysis, 5
existential frustration, 163
existentialism, ix, 3 ff., 11, 50, 73, 94
existential psychiatry, viii, 3, 6, 114, 116
existential vacuum, ix, 44–45, 59, 64-65 76, 83 ff., 96 ff., 115
Existenzanalyse, 5

NO JUNG ?

INDEX OF AUTHORS AND SOURCES